Favorite Recipes
of America's Food Editors

by the Food Editors
of America's 30 Leading Newspapers

FAVORITE RECIPES PRESS

154 East Erie Street / Chicago, Illinois 60601

CONTRIBUTING FOOD EDITORS

**ATLANTA JOURNAL
AND CONSTITUTION**
Grace Hartley
Jean Thwaite

**ARIZONA REPUBLIC
& PHOENIX GAZETTE**
Dorothee Polson
Carol M. Voshall

BALTIMORE SUNPAPERS
Martha Schoeps
Winifred Phillips

BOSTON HERALD-TRAVELER
Janet Christensen

BUFFALO NEWS
Janice Okun

CHICAGO TRIBUNE
Ruth Ellen Church

CINCINNATI ENQUIRER
Pat Williams

CLEVELAND PLAIN DEALER
Janet Beighle

DALLAS NEWS
Julie Benell

DENVER POST
Helen Dollaghan

DETROIT NEWS
Cyrilla Riley

FORT WORTH STAR-TELEGRAM
Jo Ann Vachule

HOUSTON CHRONICLE
Ann M. Criswell

INDIANAPOLIS STAR
Verna McCallum

INDIANAPOLIS NEWS
Bertha Scott

KANSAS CITY STAR & TIMES
Marjean Busby

LOS ANGELES TIMES
Jeanne Voltz

**LOUISVILLE COURIER-JOURNAL
& TIMES**
Lillian Marshall

MINNEAPOLIS STAR
Beverly Kees

MINNEAPOLIS TRIBUNE
Mary Hart

NEWARK NEWS
Joan Babbage

NEW ORLEANS TIMES-PICAYUNE
Rachel Daniel

NEW ORLEANS STATES-ITEM
Bettye Anding

NEW YORK NEWS
Alice Petersen
Ella Elvin

OAKLAND TRIBUNE
Margaret C. Bowers

PHILADELPHIA INQUIRER
Elaine Tait

PORTLAND OREGONIAN
Yvonne Rothert

OREGON JOURNAL
Marjorie Anderson

ST. LOUIS GLOBE-DEMOCRAT
Marian O'Brien

**ST. PAUL DISPATCH/
PIONEER PRESS**
Eleanor Ostman

SAN DIEGO UNION
Opal M. Crandall

SAN DIEGO EVENING TRIBUNE
Kay Jarvis

SAN FRANCISCO CHRONICLE
Jane Benet

SAN FRANCISCO EXAMINER
Helen Civelli Brown

SEATTLE TIMES
Marilyn Kirkby

WASHINGTON POST
Elinor Lee

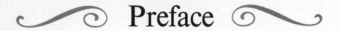 Preface

It was a great idea.
Pool the collected knowledge and experi-
ence of the 40 most famous and respected newspaper food
editors of America into one fabulous book
of recipes. Present the favorite recipes
of these renowned editors who really know cook-
ing — as professionals. That is what this book is. Here
you will not find ordinary recipes, though all are sim-
ple and practical. What you will find here are
the superb recipes, the ones that the
nation's leading newspaper food
editors have judged to be the finest recipes
in the various food categories. This is probably the most
unusual and exciting collections of recipes
ever assembled. The 300 recipes in this
book, each one with step-by-step directions, will pro-
bably become your favorites, too.

Contents

ABBREVIATIONS, SUBSTITUTIONS AND COOKING GUIDES

✻   ✻   ✻   ✻   ✻   ✻

IN MEASURING, REMEMBER. . . .

3 tsp. = 1 tbsp.	2 c. - 1 pt.
2 tbsp. = 1/8 c.	2 c. sugar = 1 lb.
4 tbsp = 1/4 c.	5/8 c. = 1/2 c. + 2 tbsp.
8 tbsp = 1/2 c.	7/8 c. = 3/4 c. + 2 tbsp.
16 tbsp. = 1 c.	1 oz. butter = 2 tbsp.
5 tbsp. + 1 tsp. = 1/3 c.	1 lb. butter = 2 c. or 4 sticks
12 tbsp. = 3/4 c.	2 pt. = 1 qt.
4 oz. = 1/2 c.	1 qt. = 4 c.
8 oz. = 1 c.	A few grains = less than 1/8 tsp.
16 oz. = 1 lb.	Pinch = as much as can be taken
1 oz. = 2 tbsp. fat or liquid	between tip of finger and thumb
2 c. fat = 1 lb.	Speck = less than 1/8 tsp.

WHEN YOU'RE MISSING AN INGREDIENT . . .

Substitute 1 teaspoon dried herbs for 1 tablespoon fresh herbs.

Try 1 cup minus 2 tablespoons all-purpose flour as a substitute for 1 cup cake flour.

Add 1/4 teaspoon baking soda and 1/2 cup buttermilk to equal 1 teaspoon baking powder. The buttermilk will replace 1/2 cup of the liquid indicated in the recipe.

Use 3 tablespoons dry cocoa plus tablespoon butter or margarine instead of 1 square (1 ounce) unsweetened chocolate.

Make custard with 1 whole egg rather than 2 egg yolks.

Mix 1/2 cup evaporated milk with 1/2 cup water (or 1 cup reconstituted nonfat dry milk with 1 tablespoon butter) to replace 1 cup whole milk.

Make 1 cup of sour milk by letting stand for 5 minutes 1 tablespoon lemon juice or vinegar plus sweet milk to make 1 cup.

Substitute 1 package (2 teaspoons) active dry yeast for 1 cake compressed yeast.

Add 1 tablespoon instant minced onion, rehydrated, to replace 1 small fresh onion.

Substitute 1 tablespoon prepared mustard for 1 teaspoon dry mustard.

Use 1/8 teaspoon garlic powder instead of 1 small pressed clove of garlic.

Substitute 2 tablespoons of flour for 1 tablespoon of cornstarch to use as a thickening agent.

Mix 1/2 cup tomato sauce with 1/2 cup of water to make 1 cup tomato juice.

Make catsup or chili with 1 cup tomato sauce plus 1/2 cup sugar and 2 tablespoons vinegar.

WHEN YOU NEED APPROXIMATE MEASUREMENTS . . .

1 lemon makes 3 tablespoons juice
1 lemon makes 1 teaspoon grated peel
1 orange makes 1/3 cup juice
1 orange makes about 2 teaspoons grated peel
1 chopped onion, medium makes 1/2 cup pieces
1 pound unshelled walnuts makes 1 1/2 to 1 3/4 cups shelled
1 pound unshelled almonds makes 3/4 to 1 cup shelled
8 to 10 egg whites make 1 cup
12 to 14 egg yolks make 1 cup
1 pound shredded American cheese makes 4 cups
1/4 pound crumbled blue cheese makes 1 cup
1 cup unwhipped cream makes 2 cups whipped
4 ounces (1 − 1 1/4 cups) uncooked macaroni makes 2 1/4 cups cooked
7 ounces spaghetti make 4 cups cooked
4 ounces (1 1/2 − 2) uncooked noodles make 2 cups cooked

OVEN TEMPERATURES

Temperature Fahrenheit	Term
250-300	Slow
325	Moderately slow
350	Moderate
375	Moderately quick
400	Moderately hot
425-450	Hot
475-500	Extremely hot

MEAT THERMOMETER TEMPERATURES

Beef
    Rare . . . . 140°
    Medium . . . . 160°
    Well-done . . . . 170°
Fresh Pork . . . . .170 - 185°
Smoked Pork
    Fully Cooked . . . . 130°
    Cook-before eating . . . . . 160°
Veal . . . . 170°
Lamb. . . . . .175 - 180°

MAKE 1 CUP OF FINE CRUMBS WITH . . .

28 saltine crackers
4 slices bread
14 square graham crackers
22 vanilla wafers

ABBREVIATIONS

Cup . . . . c.
Tablespoon. . . . . .tbsp.
Teaspoon . . . . tsp.
Pound . . . . lb.
Ounce . . . . oz.
Package . . . . pkg.
Gallon . . . . gal.
Quart . . . . qt.
Pint . . . . pt.
Dozen . . . . doz.
Large. . . . . lge.
Small. . . . . sm.

An Array of Appealing Appetizers
That Stimulate All Appetites

*E*nticing smells come from the kitchen. Your family or guests wonder what is in the offing. You appear with appetizers.

You could put an anchovy on a cracker, but for those special dinners you want something more imaginative than that. These are the most imaginative, succulent, and inviting appetizers you will ever encounter. America's foremost newspaper food editors have judged these the best.

Appetizers should whet the appetite, not dull it. They should be in harmony with what you will serve as the main course.

The appetizers that follow are guaranteed to please. For a surprise treat, try Eggplant Caviar, lucious Avocado-Louis Appetizer, South American Chili Dip, a delicious Shrimp Dip for crisp vegetables, tasty Cheese Walnuts, crisp and golden Cheese Wafers, unique Greek Shrimp and Artichokes, New Jersey's Tony Barbara's special Lobster-tail Appetizers and gourmet Sirloin Blue.

Appetizers & Accompaniments

9

AVOCADO-LOUIS APPETIZER

1 c. unflavored yogurt
1/4 c. chili sauce
1 tbsp. vinegar
1 tsp. instant minced onion
1 tsp. Worcestershire sauce
1/2 tsp. salt
Dash of liquid red pepper
1 hard-cooked egg, chopped
2 med. avocados

Combine yogurt, chili sauce, vinegar, onion, Worcestershire sauce, salt and red pepper; blend well. Chill. Spoon mixture into dish; garnish with egg. Cut avocados in halves; remove seeds. Cut fruit into balls with French ball cutter or measuring spoon; arrange around dish. Serve with cocktail picks for dipping. Yield: 8 servings.

Helen Dollaghan
The Denver Post

CHILI DIP

1/4 c. oil
1/4 c. red wine vinegar
1 lge. clove of garlic, minced
2 7-oz. cans green chilies, chopped

Mix oil, vinegar and garlic; combine with chilies. Store in refrigerator. Serve with corn chips as dip or spread.

Dorothee Polson
The Arizona Republic

GUACAMOLE DIP

3 tbsp. finely chopped onion
1 tomato, peeled and chopped
2 avocados, peeled and mashed
1 tsp. salt
2 tsp. chili powder
1 tbsp. lemon juice

Combine onion, tomato and avocados; mash until smooth. Add salt, chili powder and lemon juice; mix well. Serve as dip with corn chips.

Julie Benell
The Dallas Morning News

SHRIMP DIP

12 oz. cream cheese
2 cans broken shrimp pieces
2 tsp. lemon juice
2 tsp. minced onion
Dash of chili powder
1/8 tsp. Worcestershire sauce
1/8 tsp. garlic powder or to taste
Salt and pepper to taste

Combine all ingredients; refrigerate overnight. Serve with sliced white radishes, cucumbers, cauliflower buds, cherry tomatoes, carrots, celery and green pepper sticks.

Beverly Kees
The Minneapolis Star

Guacamole Dip
. . . an avocado party pleaser

Beer-Dip Tomatoes . . . tiny cherry tomatoes on bamboo skewers

BEER-DIP TOMATOES

1 pt. cherry tomatoes, with stems
Beer
Coarse salt

Wash, dry and chill tomatoes. To serve, dip first into beer, then into salt. Use stems as holders or use bamboo skewers.

Dorothee Polson
The Arizona Republic

CHEESE WAFERS

1 lb. sharp or med. Cheddar
  cheese, grated
1 stick less 1 tbsp. butter
1 c. flour
1/2 tsp. salt
1/2 tsp. red pepper
1 c. chopped pecans

Knead cheese with butter, flour, salt and pepper. Add pecans. Shape into roll; refrigerate overnight. Slice thin; place on cookie sheet. Bake at 325 to 350 degrees for about 10 minutes or until golden and crisp.

Jean Thwaite
The Atlanta Constitution

CHEESE WALNUTS

Sweet butter
Roquefort cheese
Walnut halves

Mash equal amounts of butter and cheese together. Spread a small amount of mixture between 2 walnut halves. Chill before serving.

Martha H. Schoeps
The Baltimore Sunpapers

EGGPLANT CAVIAR

2 lge. eggplant
Salt
Freshly ground pepper
1/2 to 1 c. salad oil
1/2 onion, coarsely chopped

Pierce eggplant with skewer to prevent bursting during baking. Place eggplant on baking sheet. Bake at 350 degrees for about 1 hour or until soft. Cool and peel. Chop pulp coarsely; season to taste with salt and pepper. Blend enough salad oil with eggplant until salad oil is absorbed. Mix in onion. Serve with black bread or wheat crackers as salad, dip or spread.

Dorothee Polson
The Arizona Republic

CRAB MEAT APPETIZER

1 8-oz. pkg. cream cheese
2 tbsp. milk
1 No. 2 can crab meat, well
    drained
3/4 c. chili sauce
Parsley or chives

Soften cream cheese with milk; mound on serving plate. Spread crab meat over cream cheese; pour chili sauce over all. Garnish with parsley. Chill for several hours. Surround by assorted crackers when ready to serve. Yield: 1-2 cups.

Patricia Williams
The Cincinnati Enquirer

GREEK SHRIMP AND ARTICHOKE APPETIZERS

1 pkg. frozen artichoke hearts
4 tbsp. oil
1 lb. fresh or frozen shrimp
1 1/4 lb. whole mushrooms
2 cloves of garlic, finely minced
1/2 tsp. salt
Pepper to taste
1/2 tsp. oregano
2 tbsp. lemon juice
1/4 c. finely chopped fresh parsley

Blanch artichoke hearts according to package directions. Heat oil in frypan; add shrimp and mushrooms. Cook, stirring frequently, until shrimp turns pink. Add artichoke hearts, garlic, salt, pepper and oregano; stir. Add lemon juice and parsley; stir to combine. Serve warm in chafing dish. Yield: About 30 appetizers.

Bertha Scott
The Indianapolis News

TONY BARBARA'S LOBSTER-TAIL APPETIZER

1 or 2 lobster-tails
Flour
1 green pepper, sliced
3 tbsp. oil
1 tbsp. butter
1/8 c. sherry
1/8 c. sauterne
1 tbsp. flavored bread crumbs

Cut lobster-tails into 1-inch pieces; coat with flour. Saute green pepper in oil and butter. Add floured lobster-tails; cook for 5 minutes. Add wines; stir in bread crumbs. Shrimp may be substituted for lobster-tails. This is an original recipe from Tony Barbara, executive chef of Governor Morris Hotel of Morristown, New Jersey.

Joan Babbage
The Newark Evening News

APPETIZER MEATBALLS

1 egg
2 slices day-old bread, cubed
2 tsp. salt
1/8 tsp. pepper
2 lb. ground beef
1/2 c. minced onion
1 12-oz. jar chili sauce
1/2 c. grape jelly
1/4 c. lemon juice
2 tbsp. vinegar

Beat egg, bread cubes, salt and pepper with rotary beater. Add ground beef and onion; mix well. Heat chili sauce, grape jelly, lemon juice and vinegar in large skillet over low heat until jelly is melted, blending well. Form beef mixture into tiny balls; place in chili sauce mixture. Cook over medium heat. Turn each meatball over in order placed in sauce. Cover; simmer for 20 minutes, stirring occasionally. Uncover; simmer for 10 minutes or until meatballs are done and sauce is thick. To serve, place in chafing dish over hot water; let guests spear meatballs with cocktail picks. May be made in advance and reheated slowly before serving. Will keep for 2 to 3 days in refrigerator; will keep for 1 month in freezer. Yield: 80-100 meatballs.

Yvonne Rothert
The Oregonian

BEEF EMPANADAS

1 lb. ground beef
1 tbsp. shortening
1 c. chopped onion
1 c. chopped fresh tomato
1/2 c. chopped green pepper
1 clove of garlic, minced
1/4 c. chopped stuffed olives
1/4 tsp. red hot sauce
1 tbsp. flour
1 1/2 tsp. salt
1/4 tsp. pepper
2   9 1/2-oz. pkg. pie crust
  mix or 1 recipe pastry
1 tbsp. water
1 egg yolk

Saute beef in shortening until lightly browned. Add onion, tomato, green pepper and garlic; cook until onion is tender, stirring often. Add olives and red hot sauce; mix. Blend in flour, salt and pepper; cook until thickened, stirring constantly. Cool. Prepare pie crust mix according to package directions. Roll out 1/8-inch thick on lightly floured board; cut into 5-inch rounds. Spoon 3 tablespoonfuls beef mixture on each crust to one side of center. Moisten edges; fold each round in half. Seal; flute edges with tines of fork. Place on ungreased baking sheet. Add water to egg yolk; beat slightly. Brush tops of pastries lightly with egg mixture. Bake at 425 degrees for 12 to 15 minutes or until crust is lightly browned. For appetizer empanadas, prepare 1/2 of the recipe. Cut crust into 3-inch rounds; fill each with 1 heaping teaspoonful beef mixture. Bake at 425 degrees for 10 to 12 minutes until browned. Yield: 4 dozen appetizer empanadas.

Janet Christensen
The Boston Herald Traveler

CHUTNEY AND HAM CANAPE

Bread rounds
Butter
Deviled ham
Chutney
Grated Parmesan cheese
Mayonnaise

Toast bread rounds on one side; butter other side. Spread buttered side with layer of deviled ham and chutney; sprinkle with cheese. Top with dollop of mayonnaise. Bake at 400 degrees until mayonnaise begins to melt; serve hot. Deviled ham may be prepared with ground leftover ham or country ham which is sauteed in butter and mixed with catsup to taste.

Marjean Phillips Busby
The Kansas City Star and Times

LIVER PASTE

2 lb. pork liver
1 lb. fat pork
1 med. onion
1/4 c. butter or margarine
1/4 c. flour
2 c. milk
2 eggs, beaten
1 tbsp. salt
1 tsp. pepper

Preheat oven to 250 degrees. Grind pork liver through grinder twice; set aside. Grind fat pork and onion through grinder twice. Melt butter in saucepan; blend in flour. Stir in milk; simmer. Add onion mixture; simmer, stirring constantly, until fat has melted. Remove from heat. Add liver, eggs, salt and pepper; stir to mix well. Pour into ovenproof baking dish; set in pan of hot water. Bake for about 1 hour and 30 minutes or until set. Serve as appetizer.

Verna McCallum
The Indianapolis Star

SMOKED SAUSAGE AND OYSTERS A LA JUSTIN WILSON

2 lb. country-smoked sausage
1 qt. med.-sized fresh oysters
2 c. sauterne or other dry
　　white wine
1 tsp. hot sauce
1/2 tsp. garlic salt
1/2 tsp. salt
Juice of 1/2 lemon

Cut sausage in 1-inch pieces. Place in large iron skillet. Add oysters and remaining ingredients. Bring to a boil; reduce heat. Simmer until most of the liquid has evaporated, leaving just enough to serve as gravy, if desired. Be sure sausage is well cooked and tender. Serve as appetizer. Yield: 6-8 servings.

Ann M. Criswell
The Houston Chronicle

SIRLOIN BLUE

1 lge. onion, chopped fine
1 1/2 lb. sirloin steak, ground twice
Salt and pepper to taste
12 oz. blue cheese
1 c. (about) beer
2 eggs, beaten
Evaporated milk
2 c. ground almonds

Grind or mix onion with steak; add salt and pepper. Form into 3/4-inch balls; refrigerate. Melt blue cheese in beer; add eggs and enough milk to make thick cheese sauce. Roll meatballs in sauce; roll in almonds. Refrigerate for 1 hour or longer. Meatballs are not cooked. May be frozen on cookie sheets; place in plastic bag in freezer. Thaw for about 20 minutes before serving. Serve as appetizer. Yield: 5-6 dozen meatballs.

Bertha Scott
The Indianapolis News

ALMOND SOUP

3　10 1/2-oz. cans beef consomme
3 c. water
1/2 c. ground almonds
1/4 c. olive oil
1/2 tsp. salt
2 c. 1/4 x 2-in. toasted bread strips
1/4 c. grated Parmesan cheese
3/4 c. toasted sliced almonds

Combine consomme and water in 3-quart saucepan; heat thoroughly. Mix ground almonds and olive oil; stir into hot consomme. Add salt. Pour soup into individual ovenproof plates or bowls. Top each serving with bread strips; sprinkle with Parmesan cheese. Place under broiler until cheese is lightly browned. Remove from broiler; sprinkle with almonds. Serve as first course soup. Yield: 6 servings.

Eleanor Ostman
The St. Paul Dispatch-Pioneer Press

Creamy Fresh Mushroom Soup
. . . a perfect first course dish

extract all liquid. Serve very hot; may be served with small circles of melba-cheese toast in demitasse cups or pots de creme for appetizer soup. Yield: 8 servings.

Marian O'Brien
The St. Louis Globe-Democrat

PUMPKIN SOUP

> *1 c. cooked rice, chilled*
> *3/4 c. half and half*
> *1/2 c. canned pumpkin*
> *2 c. chicken broth*
> *2 tsp. lemon juice*
> *2 tbsp. sugar*

Place rice and 1/2 cup half and half in blender; blend on low speed for 1 minute or until smooth. Add remaining half and half and remaining ingredients; blend on high speed. Chill for 1 hour. Yield: 4 cups.

Elaine Tait
The Philadelphia Inquirer

FRESH MUSHROOM SOUP

> *1 1/2 lb. fresh mushrooms*
> *2 tbsp. butter*
> *2 or 3 shallots, minced*
> *6 c. canned chicken broth*
> *1/2 tsp. salt*
> *1 tsp. lemon juice*
> *1 lemon, sliced*

Wash mushrooms; dry. Chop very fine or blend in blender at slow speed, small amount at a time. Heat butter in 3-quart kettle or saucepan. Add shallots; cook, stirring, for about 3 minutes or until wilted. Add mushrooms; cook, stirring occasionally, for about 5 minutes. Add broth, salt and lemon juice; bring to a boil. Reduce heat; simmer, uncovered, for 30 minutes. Serve garnished with lemon slices. If smooth soup is preferred, blend finished soup in blender for moment or press through coarse sieve, pressing mushrooms hard enough to

SALAD SOUP

> *1 sm. clove of garlic, mashed*
> *1 tbsp. sugar*
> *1 1/2 tsp. salt*
> *1 46-oz. can tomato juice*
> *1/4 c. salad oil*
> *2 tbsp. lemon juice*
> *1 tsp. Worcestershire sauce*
> *3 tomatoes, finely diced*
> *1 cucumber, finely diced*
> *1 green pepper, finely diced*
> *1 c. shredded carrots*
> *1 c. thinly sliced celery*
> *1/4 c. thinly sliced green onion*

Mix garlic, sugar, salt, tomato juice, oil, lemon juice and Worcestershire sauce. Stir in vegetables; chill. Serve in chilled dishes with sesame crackers; keeps for several days, if refrigerated. Use as first course soup. Yield: 10-12 servings.

Mary Hart
The Minneapolis Tribune

GAZPACHO

1/4 lge. green pepper, seeds removed
2 ripe tomatoes, quartered
1/4 sm. onion, sliced
1/2 cucumber, sliced
1/2 garlic clove, peeled
1/8 tsp. red hot sauce
1/2 tsp. salt
1 tbsp. olive oil
4 1/2 tsp. wine vinegar
1/4 c. ice water

Slice green pepper; place in blender. Add remaining ingredients; cover. Blend for 3 seconds or until of serving consistency; chill. To serve, pour into soup plates with 1 ice cube in center of each; garnish with sour cream and avocado slices, if desired. Serve as first course soup. Yield: 3 servings.

Jane Benet
The San Francisco Chronicle

TURTLE SOUP

1 1/2 lb. turtle meat
1 tbsp. shortening
1 tbsp. flour
1 onion, chopped
1 8-oz. can tomato sauce
2 hard-cooked eggs
3 tbsp. olive oil
1 tsp. ground cloves
1/2 tsp. nutmeg
1 tsp. cinnamon
1/2 lemon, sliced
3 cloves of garlic, crushed
1/2 c. sherry

Cut meat into small pieces; boil in salted water until tender. Drain; reserve liquid. Remove meat from bones; cut into smaller pieces. Melt shortening; add flour. Brown over low heat as for roux, stirring constantly; add onion. Stir in tomato sauce. Combine egg yolks, olive oil, cloves, nutmeg and cinnamon; add to tomato mixture. Combine turtle meat and reserved liquid in saucepan; stir in tomato mix-

ture. Bring to a boil; simmer for 40 minutes. Add lemon and garlic; simmer for 20 minutes longer. Season to taste. Add sherry and thinly sliced egg whites just before serving. If turtle has eggs, boil in soup for added flavor.

Rachel Daniel
The New Orleans Times-Picayune

FRESH PINEAPPLE CHUTNEY

2 med. pineapples
2 onions, chopped
2 c. raisins
1 c. currants
1/2 c. chopped preserved ginger
3 c. brown sugar
3 c. cider vinegar
1 tsp. salt
1/2 tsp. each cinnamon, cloves
   and allspice
1/4 tsp. cayenne
1/4 tsp. pepper

Peel pineapple; remove core. Cut pineapple into chunks. Combine all ingredients in enamel kettle. Simmer until liquid has almost evaporated, stirring occasionally. Cover; let stand overnight. Reheat to boiling point. Pour into hot sterilized jars. Seal.

Alice Petersen
The New York News

RHUBARB JAM

5 c. rhubarb
4 c. sugar
1 3-oz. pkg. strawberry gelatin
Paraffin

Wash rhubarb; trim leaves and blemishes. Split down length if stalks are wide. Cut rhubarb into 1 1/2-inch crosswise slices. Place in large glass bowl; add sugar. Cover; leave at room temperature overnight, stirring occasionally. Bring rapidly to boiling point; boil for 10 minutes. Skim white foam from surface; remove from heat. Stir in gelatin until dissolved; ladle into scalded jelly glasses. Cover with paraffin; label jars. Yield: Four 8-ounce glasses.

Verna McCallum
The Indianapolis Star

PICKLED EGGS

2 No. 303 cans sm. whole beets,
*   drained and juice reserved*
2 doz. hard-cooked eggs, peeled
1 c. sugar
2 c. vinegar
2 tbsp. pickling spices

Place beets and eggs in large container. Mix reserved beet juice, sugar and vinegar in saucepan. Place spices in small piece of cloth; tie tightly. Add to vinegar mixture; bring to a rolling boil. Remove from heat; let set for 20 minutes. Remove spice bag; pour over egg mixture. Cool; cover. Refrigerate for at least 3 days before serving.

Grace Hartley
The Atlanta Journal

HOT SPICED FRUIT

1   16-oz. can pear halves
1   1-lb. 4-oz. can pineapple spears
1   16-oz. can peach halves
1   1-lb. 1-oz. can figs
1 tbsp. brown sugar
1/4 c. butter
1 tsp. curry powder
1 tsp. cinnamon
1/2 tsp. nutmeg

Drain fruits; dry. Place in 10 x 6 x 2-inch baking dish, placing pears and pineapple in center and peaches and figs at either end. Sprinkle with sugar; dot with butter. Sprinkle with spices. Bake for 50 minutes at 325 degrees. Serve from baking dish with ham, lamb or poultry. May be prepared without figs with maraschino cherries added for color. Yield: 12 servings.

Marjean Phillips Busby
The Kansas City Star and Times

MOTHER'S PEAR HONEY

5 c. coarsely ground Kieffer pears
*   or any firm unripe pears*
10 c. sugar
2 c. crushed pineapple

Peel and core pears. Put pears through food grinder, using coarse blade. Combine pears, sugar and pineapple in 5-quart pan. Cook about 30 to 45 minutes or until mixture is thick and pears are clear. Pour into jars and seal. Yield: About 7 pints.

Marjean Phillips Busby
The Kansas City Star and Times

MINTED MELON

1/2 c. sugar
1/2 c. water
3 tbsp. chopped mint leaves
Juice of 1 lemon
Juice of 1 orange
Honeydew melon balls, chilled

Boil sugar and water for 5 minutes; pour over mint leaves. Cool; strain. Add to lemon and orange juices; chill. Place melon balls in cocktail glasses; pour syrup over melon balls. Garnish with sprigs of mint.

Jo Ann Vachule
The Fort Worth Star-Telegram

SWEET PEPPER RELISH

12 green bell peppers
12 red bell peppers
7 med. onions
3 c. vinegar
3 c. sugar
2 tbsp. salt
2 tbsp. mustard seed

Grind peppers and onions; combine with vegetable juices and remaining ingredients. Boil for 30 minutes; pour into hot sterilized jars. Seal. Yield: About 4 quarts.

Kay Jarvis
The San Diego Evening Tribune

Beautiful Salads and Delicious Dressings
to Brighten the Appetite

S alads have become an American specialty. With
year-round growing seasons in Florida, Texas,
and California, there are always crisp, green heads of
lettuce, crunchy peppers, red tomatoes, and other
fresh vegetables in our stores from coast to coast.

Grandma served salads in the summer when the crops
ripened. Today you can serve a salad as easily and
conveniently on Christmas Day as you can on the Fourth
of July.

American restaurants usually serve the salad before
the main course; most European restaurants serve the
salad after the main course. Regardless of when you
choose to serve it, your salad will add color, piquancy,
and freshness to your meal.

Make your choice from among the great salads which have
been contributed by America's leading food editors.
Included are such superlative salad recipes as Crab Louis,
Blueberry Salad, Cranberry Mold, Corned Beef in Aspic,
Green Goddess Salad, and Marinated Artichoke Hearts Ivar.

19

BLUEBERRY SALAD

1 envelope plain gelatin
1/4 c. cold water
3/4 c. sugar
1/2 pt. cream
1 c. sour cream
1 tsp. vanilla
1 pkg. any flavor red gelatin
1 c. boiling water
1 15-oz. can blueberries, undrained
Whipped cream or whipped topping
Maraschino cherries

Soften gelatin in cold water. Combine sugar and cream in saucepan; bring to boiling point. Remove from heat; stir in gelatin, sour cream and vanilla. Pour into mold or 6 x 10-inch dish. Chill until firm. Mix red gelatin with boiling water until dissolved. Add blueberries; cool. Pour over first mixture. Chill until firm. Serve with whipped cream, topped with maraschino cherries. Yield: 8 servings.

Bertha Scott
The Indianapolis News

CELESTIAL PEACH SALAD

1 envelope plain gelatin
4 tbsp. lemon juice
3/4 c. peach syrup
1/4 tsp. salt
1/2 c. mayonnaise
1 3-oz. pkg. cream cheese
2/3 c. chilled evaporated milk
6 canned cling peach halves

Soften gelatin in lemon juice. Heat peach syrup; add gelatin and stir until dissolved. Blend in salt; cool to room temperature. Blend mayonnaise and cream cheese together; gradually blend in gelatin mixture. Whip evaporated milk until light and fluffy; fold into gelatin mixture. Dice enough peaches to make 1 cup; add to mixture. Place 1 peach half, cup-side down, in 1-quart mold; pour gelatin mixture over top. Chill until firm. Unmold; garnish with remaining peach halves, cut into quarters. Yield: 6 servings.

Margaret C. Bowers
The Oakland Tribune

CRANBERRY MOLD

1 lb. ground fresh cranberries
1 c. sugar
1 lb. miniature marshmallows
2 1/2 c. drained crushed pineapple
1 pt. whipping cream, whipped
1 c. chopped walnuts

Combine cranberries, sugar, marshmallows and pineapple; cover. Refrigerate overnight. Fold in whipped cream and walnuts. Pour into four 1-quart molds; freeze until firm. May serve in sherbet glasses for dessert before freezing, if desired.

Dorothy Neighbors
The Seattle Times

FRESH FRUIT SALAD

Fresh grapefruit sections
Fresh orange sections
Fresh strawberries or cherries
Sour cream
Nutmeg or cinnamon

Combine grapefruit sections, orange sections and strawberries; add enough sour cream to coat well. Chill before serving. Sprinkle nutmeg over individual servings.

Martha H. Schoeps
The Baltimore Sun

ORANGE-PINEAPPLE-APRICOT SALAD

2 pkg. orange gelatin
2 c. hot water
3/4 c. marshmallows
1/2 c. pineapple juice
1/2 c. apricot juice
1 No. 2 1/2 can pineapple tidbits
1 No. 2 1/2 can apricots, cut up
Topping
Grated cheese (opt.)

Dissolve gelatin in hot water. Add marshmallows; stir until melted. Add pineapple and apricot juices; chill until partially congealed. Add pineapple and apricots; chill until firm. Add Topping; sprinkle with grated cheese.

TOPPING

1/2 c. sugar
1/2 c. pineapple juice
3 tbsp. flour
1 egg
1/2 c. apricot juice
2 tbsp. butter
1 c. whipping cream, whipped

Combine first 6 ingredients in saucepan; bring to a boil. Let cool; fold in whipped cream

Jean Thwaite
The Atlanta Constitution

CRAB LOUIS

1/2 med. head lettuce, shredded
1 1/2 c. cooked crab meat, chilled
1 lge. tomato, cut into wedges
2 hard-cooked eggs, sliced
8 ripe olives, pitted
Pimento strips
Louis Dressing

Arrange lettuce in 4 individual serving bowls; mound crab meat on lettuce. Garnish with tomato wedges, egg slices, olives and pimento strips; chill. Spoon Louis Dressing over salad just before serving.

LOUIS DRESSING

1 c. mayonnaise
1/2 c. chili sauce
1 1/2 tsp. grated onion
1 tsp. horseradish
1 tsp. lemon juice
1/4 tsp. crushed dried tarragon
1/4 tsp. salt
1/8 tsp. white pepper

Mix all ingredients. Serve as luncheon main dish or as 8 individual side salads.

Crab Louis originated in San Francisco and along the Pacific Coast and is made preferably with fresh Dungeness crab, but any good quality crab, fresh, frozen or canned, may be substituted.

Helen Civelli Brown
The San Francisco Examiner

Curried Salmon Salad

CURRIED SALMON SALAD

1 1-lb. can salmon
1 1/2 c. chopped celery
2 green onions, sliced thin
3 hard-cooked eggs, sliced
1 c. fresh or frozen peas, cooked
1/2 c. mayonnaise
1/2 c. sour cream
1 tbsp. lemon juice
1 1/2 tsp. (or more) curry powder
1 1/2 tsp. salt
1/4 tsp. pepper

Flake salmon; place in bowl with celery, onions, eggs and peas, reserving small amount of peas and half the egg slices for garnish. Blend remaining ingredients; toss lightly with salmon mixture. Serve on lettuce; garnish with reserved peas, egg slices and tomato wedges. Yield: 6 servings.

Ruth Ellen Church
The Chicago Tribune

21

NORTHWEST SEAFOOD

1 lge. loaf sliced white sandwich
  bread
Butter
1 lge. onion
4 hard-cooked eggs
2 5-oz. cans sm. shrimp, drained
1 7 1/2-oz. can crab meat
1 c. finely cubed celery
3 c. mayonnaise
Salad greens
Crisp cucumber slices
Cherry tomatoes

Cut crusts from bread; spread slices lightly with butter. Cut each slice into 20 cubes. Combine finely chopped onion and eggs with bread cubes. Refrigerate overnight. Add shrimp, crab meat, celery and mayonnaise; mix lightly. Cover; let stand for 3 or 4 hours in refrigerator before serving. Pile lightly on salad greens; garnish with cucumber and cherry tomatoes. Surprise ingredient in this salad is the bread cubes. Let stand overnight for best results. Yield: 12 servings.

Marjorie Anderson "Mary Cullen"
The Oregon Journal

CORNED BEEF IN ASPIC

1 12-oz. can corned beef
1 tbsp. unflavored gelatin
1/4 c. cold water
2 10 1/2-oz. cans beef consomme
2 tbsp. sherry
Salad greens
3 hard-cooked eggs, sliced
1 tbsp. tarragon vinegar
1/2 c. mayonnaise

Flake corned beef with fork into bite-sized pieces; refrigerate while preparing aspic mixture. Soften gelatin in water. Heat 1 can consomme to boiling point. Dissolve gelatin in hot consomme. Add remaining consomme and sherry; chill until partially thickened. Fold in corned beef; turn into six

5-ounce molds or custard cups. Chill until firm. Loosen edges of each mold; turn out on salad greens. Top each serving with center slice from eggs. Press remaining eggs through coarse sieve; arrange around molds as garnish. Blend vinegar and mayonnaise; serve as dressing for molds. Yield: 6 servings.

Helen Dollaghan
The Denver Post

BAKED HAM SALAD

3 c. diced cooked ham
1 c. diced celery
1/2 c. chopped stuffed olives
2 hard-cooked eggs, diced
1/4 c. chopped onion
1 tbsp. lemon juice
1 tbsp. prepared mustard
Dash of pepper
3/4 c. mayonnaise
1 c. crushed potato chips

Combine ham, celery, olives, eggs, onion, lemon juice, mustard, pepper and mayonnaise. Place in greased casserole; top with crushed potato chips. Bake at 400 degrees for 15 to 20 minutes or until heated through. Yield: 6 servings.

Cyrilla Riley
The Detroit News

BUFFET CHICKEN SALAD

2 c. cooked cubed chicken
3/4 c. chopped celery
1/2 c. blanched almonds, toasted
2 tbsp. chopped green olives
2 tbsp. chopped ripe olives
2 hard-cooked eggs, sliced
1/8 tsp. poultry seasoning or to
  taste
1/4 tsp. salt
Sm. amount of chopped onion
Garlic powder to taste
Lemon juice or Italian dressing
1/2 c. heavy mayonnaise

Combine first 10 ingredients; toss lightly. Stir enough lemon juice into mayonnaise to thin; toss with chicken mixture. Chill. Yield: 6 servings.

Verna McCallum
The Indianapolis Star

CHICKEN-FRUIT SALAD

2 c. cooked chicken, cubed
2 med. oranges, sectioned
1/4 c. grapes, halved
1/4 c. salted almonds, chopped
1 banana, sliced
Mayonnaise
Pineapple rings

Combine chicken, oranges, grapes, almonds and banana with enough mayonnaise to bind. Make triangle with 3 pineapple rings on each plate; pile salad on top. All ingredients except banana may be prepared in advance and combined just before serving. Yield: 6 servings.

Beverly Kees
The Minneapolis Star

WALNUT-CHICKEN CONDIMENT SALAD

2/3 c. chopped toasted walnuts
2 c. cubed cooked chicken
1/4 c. finely chopped celery
2 tbsp. chopped green onion
2 tbsp. chopped raisins
2 tbsp. chopped chutney
1/4 c. mayonnaise
1/4 tsp. salt
2 tsp. lemon juice
Lettuce
4 slices tomato
4 slices pineapple, drained
Toasted walnut halves (opt.)

Combine chopped walnuts, chicken, celery and onion. Stir raisins, chutney, mayonnaise, salt and lemon juice together; fold into chicken mixture. Arrange crisp lettuce on chilled salad plates. Center each portion of lettuce with tomato slice; top with pineapple slice. Divide chicken salad into 4 equal portions; pile or scoop on top of each pineapple slice. Garnish with walnut halves. May be served with additional mayonnaise. To toast walnuts, drop kernels into rapidly boiling water; boil for 3 minutes. Drain well; spread evenly in shallow pan. Bake at 350 degrees, stirring often, for about 10 minutes or until lightly browned. Yield: 4 servings.

Eleanor Ostman
The St. Paul Dispatch-Pioneer Press

TURKEY SALAD

2 1/2 qt. diced cooked turkey or
  chicken
3 c. sliced celery
1/4 c. chopped onion
1 c. diced watermelon pickles
4 tsp. salt
2 c. mayonnaise
2 tbsp. lemon juice

Combine all ingredients; toss lightly. Serve on crisp greens. Smaller portions may be served in avocado halves or whole tomatoes. One cup toasted slivered almonds may be added, if desired. Yield: 24 servings.

Ruth Ellen Church
The Chicago Tribune

CUCUMBER SALAD

2 med. cucumbers
1 sm. peeled red onion
2 tsp. salt
3 tbsp. each vinegar and water
1/2 tsp. sugar
1/4 tsp. each paprika and pepper
1 c. sour cream

Peel cucumbers and onion; slice both thin. Separate onion into rings. Combine cucumbers, onion and salt; let stand for 30 minutes. Squeeze out liquid; place in bowl. Combine remaining ingredients; pour over cucumbers and onion. Chill until serving time.

Janet Beighle
The Cleveland Plain Dealer

maining garlic oil; drain. Mix croutons into salad just before serving. Reserve remaining garlic oil for future use. Yield: 8-10 servings.

Margaret C. Bowers
The Oakland Tribune

CAESAR SALAD

4 cloves of garlic, cut up
1 c. olive oil
2 med. heads lettuce, broken up
*   or 3 qt. salad greens*
1/2 c. unseasoned olive oil
1 tbsp. Worcestershire sauce
1/2 tsp. dry mustard
Salt and pepper to taste
1/2 c. Romanello cheese, grated
1/4 c. crumbled Roquefort cheese
1 egg, unbeaten
1/2 c. lemon juice
2 c. crisp croutons

Combine garlic and 1 cup oil; let stand at room temperature for several hours. Place lettuce in large salad bowl. Remove garlic from oil. Combine 1/4 cup garlic oil with 1/2 cup unseasoned olive oil; pour over lettuce. Sprinkle lettuce with Worcestershire sauce, mustard, salt, pepper and cheeses; toss lightly. Break egg on salad; pour on lemon juice. Mix and toss, coating each lettuce leaf. Dip croutons in re-

YOLANDE BAVAN'S CUCUMBER AND YOGURT SALAD

1 cucumber
Salt to taste
Ginger powder to taste
Garlic to taste
Minced fresh dillweed or dill
*   powder to taste*
Curry powder to taste
Yogurt, plain

Peel cucumber; dice into small cubes. Place in wooden bowl. Sprinkle with salt, ginger powder, crushed garlic, minced dillweed and curry powder. Toss. Refrigerate until 15 minutes before serving. Add yogurt to desired consistency; mix well. Add more salt if needed. Miss Bavan, an actress and singer from Ceylon, is a very enthusiastic cook.

Joan Babbage
The Newark Evening News

DIETER'S SALAD

Several varieties of lettuce--
*   Bibb, romaine, head, leaf,*
*   endive, etc.*
Rice vinegar
Sesame salt

Arrange lettuce in attractive pattern in salad bowl. Serve rice vinegar and sesame salt on side. There are almost no calories but vinegar and sesame salt provide enough flavor that the dieter feels less sorry for himself.

Beverly Kees
The Minneapolis Star

GREEN GODDESS SALAD

6 c. bite-sized pieces romaine,
  chilled
3 c. torn curly endive
1/2 lb. cooked sm. shrimp
1 clove of garlic, cut up
1 c. mayonnaise
1/2 c. sour cream
1/3 c. chopped parsley
3 tbsp. minced chives
1 to 3 tbsp. anchovy paste
3 tbsp. tarragon vinegar
1 tbsp. lemon juice
Dash of freshly ground pepper
Tomato wedges

Place romaine, endive and shrimp in large bowl. Rub small bowl with garlic. Add mayonnaise, sour cream, parsley, chives, anchovy paste, vinegar, lemon juice and pepper. Mix well; refrigerate for 1 hour. Drizzle 1/3 cup dressing over salad in bowl; toss until each leaf is well coated with dressing. Garnish with tomato wedges. Serve on chilled salad plates with remaining dressing. Yield: 6-8 servings.

Jeanne Voltz
The Los Angeles Times

INSALATA VERDE CON SALSICCIA

GREEN SALAD WITH SAUSAGE

1 c. finely diced soft salami or
  summer sausage
1 15-oz. can artichoke hearts,
  well drained and quartered
1/4 lb. fresh mushrooms, sliced,
  or 1 4-oz. can sliced
  mushrooms
1 sm. sweet red onion, sliced
  thin and separated in rings
1 8-oz. bottle Italian dressing
1 qt. Bibb lettuce, Boston lettuce
  or other tender greens
1 qt. bitter greens, such as
  dandelion, curly endive,
  escarole or watercress

Buy whole sausage or chunk; do not use ready-sliced kind. Mix first 4 ingredients. Shake bottle of dressing; pour over salami mixture. Cover; marinate for several hours in refrigerator. Wash greens; dry well. Break or tear tender greens into salad bowl; clip bitter greens with kitchen scissors into bite-sized pieces into bowl. Drain Italian dressing from marinated ingredients; pour dressing over greens, tossing gently to coat well. Mix in marinated ingredients; serve at table with hot buttered French bread or dark rye. Sprinkle with Parmesan cheese, if desired. Salad is best made with new young dandelion greens; plant is tenderest before it develops buds. Dandelion greens take lots of washing, but salad is worth the work. Yield: 4 luncheon-size servings.

Ruth Ellen Church
The Chicago Tribune

MARINATED ARTICHOKE HEARTS IVAR

4 green bell peppers
4 red bell peppers
1/2 c. cold water
1 clove of garlic
1 jar marinated artichoke hearts,
  cut up
Salt and pepper to taste
Vinegar to taste

Place peppers in a shallow pan. Bake in 400-degree oven for 30 minutes or until peppers are soft and skin begins to shrivel. Remove peppers from oven; place in deep bowl. Pour cold water over peppers. Cover with dish towel for 20 minutes. Remove as much skin as possible from peppers; chop with garlic. Add artichoke hearts. Season with salt, pepper and vinegar. Mix well; return to refrigerator until cold and ready to serve. Yield: 4-6 servings.

Helen Civelli Brown
The San Francisco Examiner

NEW ORLEANS BROCCOLI MOLD

2   10-oz. pkg. frozen chopped
    broccoli
2 tbsp. unflavored gelatin
1   10-oz. can consomme
2 tbsp. lemon juice
1 tsp. red hot sauce
1/2 tsp. salt
1/2 c. mayonnaise
3 hard-cooked eggs, chopped

Cook broccoli according to package directions. Soak gelatin in 1/2 cup consomme for 5 minutes. Heat remaining consomme. Add to gelatin mixture; stir to dissolve. Drain broccoli; chop into smaller pieces, if necessary. Combine with lemon juice, red hot sauce, salt, mayonnaise and eggs. Pour half the consomme mixture into 6-cup ring mold; chill until set. Add remaining consomme mixture to broccoli mixture; pour over congealed layer. Chill until firm. Unmold onto platter of salad greens; garnish with deviled eggs and tomato wedges. Yield: 8-10 servings.

Bertha Scott
The Indianapolis News

PIQUANTE LIMA BEANS

1 1/2 pkg. frozen lima beans
1 c. celery, diced
1 dill pickle, diced
4 green onions and tops, chopped
1/2 c. sour cream
1/4 c. mayonnaise
2 tbsp. lemon juice
2 tbsp. horseradish mustard or
    mustard with 1 tsp.
    horseradish added

Cook lima beans according to package directions; drain. Mix remaining ingredients; toss with beans. Let stand for 8 hours or longer. Yield: 6-8 servings.

Opal M. Crandall
The San Diego Union

REFRIGERATOR COLESLAW

1 med. head cabbage, shredded
1 tsp. salt
1 mango pepper, shredded
1 carrot, shredded
1/2 c. vinegar
1/2 c. water
2 c. sugar
1 tsp. celery seed
1 tsp. mustard seed

Combine cabbage and salt. Allow to stand for 1 hour. Squeeze out liquid. Add mango pepper and carrot. Combine remaining ingredients; boil for 1 minute. Cool. Pour over cabbage mixture. Will keep well in refrigerator 3 weeks or may be frozen.

Verna McCallum
The Indianapolis Star

SPICY CAULIFLOWER

1 lge. head cauliflower
1/2 tsp. pickling spice
1 tsp. salt
1/2 c. boiling water
1 tbsp. chopped anchovies
1/4 c. salad oil
2 tbsp. lemon juice
4 red onion rings
1/3 c. sliced green olives

Wash cauliflower. Cut off base; separate into flowerets. Add pickling spice and salt to boiling water; add cauliflower. Cover; cook until crisp-tender, about 5 minutes. Drain. Mash anchovies. Add oil and lemon juice; mix. Pour over hot cauliflower; toss. Refrigerate for at least 1 hour. Garnish with onion rings and olives. Serve on lettuce. Yield: 4-6 servings.

Janice Okun
The Buffalo Evening News

MAYFAIR DRESSING

1 button of garlic
1 rib celery
1/2 med. onion

1 2-oz. can flat anchovies
1 tsp. ground pepper
1 tsp. (heaping) monosodium
     glutamate
1/2 tsp. sugar
2 tbsp. salad mustard
1 tbsp. lemon juice
3 eggs
2 c. salad oil

Peel and slice garlic; scrape and slice celery. Peel and slice onion. Place in blender; add remaining ingredients except eggs and salad oil. Whirl with on-and-off rhythm for about 2 seconds. Add eggs, one at a time; whirl for several seconds after each addition. Add oil, one tablespoon at a time, blending after each addition, until one cup is used. Add remaining oil, quarter cup at a time; blend for several seconds after all oil has been added. Keeps for week or longer in refrigerator. Featured in Mayfair Room at Mayfair Hotel in St. Louis. Yield: 1 quart.

Marian O'Brien
The St. Louis Globe-Democrat

SPECIAL FRUIT SAUCE

1/2 c. honey
1/2 c. water
3 cardamom seeds, peeled and
     crushed fine
1/2 tsp. salt
6 to 8 mint leaves, crushed
1 tbsp. lemon juice
1/2 c. sherry or port wine

Mix honey, water and cardamom seeds; simmer for 5 minutes. Add salt and mint leaves; cool. Strain; add lemon juice and sherry. Pour over chilled fruit; serve. Cantaloupe balls, honeydew melon balls and blueberries are good combination for chilled fruits; sauce is excellent on grapefruit segments. Yield: About 6 servings.

Mary Hart
The Minneapolis Tribune

Blender Poppy Seed Dressing
. . . a perfect accent for fresh fruits

BLENDER POPPY SEED DRESSING

3/4 c. sugar
1 tsp. dry mustard
1 tsp. salt
1 sm. slice onion
1/3 c. vinegar
1 c. salad oil
1 tbsp. poppy seeds

Combine sugar, mustard, salt, onion and vinegar in blender container; whirl to blend. Add oil gradually while beating at low speed. Stir in poppy seeds; refrigerate. Serve on fruit salads.

Patricia Williams
The Cincinnati Enquirer

27

Hearty Beef, Pork, Lamb and Veal plus a Selection of Wild Game and Variety Meats

A ny man considers meat to be the cornerstone of a meal. Meat contains body-building, strength-giving protein.

Nearly every kind of meat the world knows is available in America. Great American cooks have borrowed from the meat cookery traditions of Europe and Asia, and have gone beyond them to develop special techniques of their own. American cooks can make a Fondue Bourguignon in the French style or broil a hearty steak over an outdoor grill with no more seasoning than salt and pepper.

The collection of meat recipes which follows includes the favorites of America's leading food experts. Here you will find Girard's Steak Diane, Sauerbraten, Beef Wellington and Daube. You will find a very special New England Boiled Dinner and a delicious Veal Mousse with Supreme Sauce, a rare recipe for Cleo Johns' Pork Crown Roast with Cranberries, Honey-Sherry Glazed Spareribs, and English Sausage Rolls plus many more.

Meats

29

DAUBE

1/4 lb. salt pork
Salt and pepper
3 lge. onions
2 bay leaves
1 clove of garlic
Thyme and cloves
1 5-lb. beef round roast
1 tbsp. shortening
2 tbsp. minced parsley
2 turnips, diced
5 carrots, diced
1 c. sherry
Cayenne pepper

Cut pork into thin shreds; rub with salt and pepper. Chop 1 onion, 1 bay leaf, garlic, thyme and cloves; mix thoroughly. Make incisions about 3 or 4 inches long in beef roast. Insert pieces of salt pork; add seasoning mixture. Brown roast in shortening in heavy saucepan. Chop remaining onions finely; add to roast. Add remaining bay leaf, parsley, turnips and carrots. Cover tightly; simmer for 10 minutes. Cover with 1 quart boiling water; add sherry, salt, pepper and cayenne. Cover; simmer for 3 hours or until tender. Yield: 10 servings.

Rachel Daniel
The New Orleans Times-Picayune

BELGIAN BEER STEW

1 3-lb. beef chuck roast
1 smoked ham hock
1/2 c. oil
2 1/2 tsp. salt
1 lge. onion, thinly sliced
2 beef bouillon cubes
1 c. boiling water
3 tbsp. flour
Beer, at room temperature
1/2 tsp. pepper
2 tsp. sugar
2 tbsp. parsley flakes
Pinch each of marjoram, thyme
    and rosemary
1 clove of garlic, chopped fine

4 carrots
3/4 c. walnuts
2 tbsp. red wine vinegar
2 tbsp. Scotch whiskey

Cut beef into 1 x 2-inch strips. Remove ham from bone; cut into 1/2-inch cubes. Brown beef and ham in oil in large skillet. Remove meat; sprinkle with 1 teaspoon salt. Set aside. Brown onion in same oil; set aside. Dissolve bouillon cubes in boiling water; let cool. Drain off and reserve all but 3 tablespoons oil in skillet. Stir flour into oil to make light brown roux. Add 1 1/2 cups beer gradually, stirring until mixture boils. Add bouillon, remaining salt, pepper, sugar, herbs and garlic. Cut carrots into 1-inch pieces. Alternate layers of meat, onion and carrots in large casserole; add sauce and enough more beer to cover meat. Bake, covered, in 300-degree oven for 2 hours and 30 minutes. Add beer, as needed. Saute walnuts in reserved oil until crisp. Add to stew. Bake for 10 to 15 minutes longer. Add vinegar and Scotch whiskey before serving. Yield: 8 servings.

Beverly Kees
The Minneapolis Star

SWEET AND SOUR POT ROAST

1 3 1/2-lb. chuck roast
Flour
Salt, pepper and paprika to taste
1 No. 2 can whole tomatoes
Juice of 1 lemon or to taste
3 tbsp. sugar or to taste

Cut roast into small chunks; roll in mixture of flour, salt, pepper and paprika. Brown in small amount of fat in heavy pot. Pour tomatoes over meat; season with lemon juice and sugar. Cover; cook over low heat for about 3 hours or until meat is tender. Yield: 6 servings.

Grace Hartley
The Atlanta Journal

Beef Wellington . . . a superb gourmet entree

BEEF WELLINGTON

1 4-lb. (about) beef fillet
Salt and pepper
1/2 stick softened butter
1/2 c. each chopped onion,
    carrot and celery
Thyme
Rosemary
Suet
2 tbsp. butter
1/2 lb. chicken livers
4 tbsp. minced shallots
1/2 c. dry sherry
Worcestershire sauce (opt.)
2 pkg. crescent refrigerator
    dinner rolls
1 egg yolk, beaten
Sauce Madere

Trim fillet; fold small end underneath to make even piece of beef. Season with salt and pepper; rub with softened butter. Place in baking pan. Top with onion, carrot and celery; sprinkle generously with thyme and rosemary. Arrange thin slices of suet on top to avoid basting. Bake at 425 degrees for 25 minutes. Remove from oven. Discard suet; reserve baked vegetables for Sauce Madere. Let fillet cool. Melt 2 tablespoons butter in small skillet. Add chicken livers; cook, stirring, until all pink color has disappeared. Add shallots and sherry; cook until most of the sherry has disappeared. Place chicken liver mixture in blender container; blend to make a paste. Season with salt, pepper and a small amount of Worcestershire sauce; spread over fillet. Chill again. Spread refrigerator rolls on board, pressing dough together where divided. Wrap fillet in dough; press together at seams. Trim off excess dough. Brush with egg yolk. Decorate with cutouts of leftover dough. Bake for 25 minutes at 425 degrees. Reduce oven temperature to 375 degrees; bake for 25 minutes more. Let fillet rest for at least 25 minutes before serving. Carve fillet with serrated knife as pastry will crumble slightly. Serve with Sauce Madere. Yield: 8 servings.

SAUCE MADERE

2 c. beef bouillon
1 tbsp. tomato paste
Reserved baked vegetables
2 tsp. cornstarch
1/4 c. dry sherry

Combine bouillon, tomato paste and reserved vegetables in saucepan; simmer for 30 minutes. Combine cornstarch and sherry; stir in bouillon mixture. Cook until thick.

Marian O'Brien
The St. Louis Globe-Democrat

◄ *Sauerbraten*
. . .a long-time German specialty

very tender. Remove beef. Strain stock, reserving 3 cups liquid. Melt butter in saucepan; stir in flour. Stir in stock, slowly; simmer until slightly thickened. Add gingersnaps and raisins; cook until sauce is thickened. Add sugar to taste. Shoulder of pork or fresh ham may be substituted for beef, if desired.

Martha H. Schoeps
The Baltimore Sun

GRILLADES

> *1 round steak*
> *Salt and pepper to taste*
> *Cayenne pepper to taste*
> *1 tbsp. shortening*
> *1 lge. onion, chopped*
> *1 clove of garlic*
> *1 tbsp. flour*
> *2 tomatoes, sliced*
> *1/2 tbsp. vinegar*
> *1 c. hot water*

Pound round steak well. Cut into grillades about 4 inches square; season highly with salt, pepper and cayenne pepper. Heat shortening in frying pan. Add onion and garlic; cook until brown. Add flour to make a brown roux. Add tomatoes with juice; arrange grillades on top. Cover; let cook until brown on one side. Turn; add vinegar and water. Stir well. Let simmer slowly, for about 30 minutes. This is a traditional creole breakfast dish and is still served at Sunday brunch and midnight breakfasts.

Bettye Anding
The New Orleans States-Item

BEEF ROLLS IN CREAM

> *2 lb. beef round steak*
> *Salt and pepper*
> *1/4 lb. fresh pork fat*

SAUERBRATEN

> *1   3 1/2 to 4-lb. boned rump*
> *or shoulder of beef*
> *1 qt. buttermilk*
> *Several drops of lemon juice*
> *2 c. red wine*
> *2 c. water*
> *1 tbsp. salt*
> *1 bay leaf*
> *4 or 5 peppercorns*
> *1 tbsp. vinegar*
> *3 tbsp. butter*
> *3 tbsp. flour*
> *1/2 c. crushed gingersnaps*
> *1/4 c. raisins or currants*
> *Sugar to taste (opt.)*

Wash and dry beef. Place in deep bowl; cover with buttermilk and lemon juice. Marinate in refrigerator for 2 days, turning several times. Remove; wash off buttermilk. Place beef in pot or kettle; add wine, water, salt, bay leaf, peppercorns and vinegar. Cook, covered, for about 3 hours or until

3 tbsp. butter or margarine
1 tbsp. flour
1 1/2 c. (about) beef broth
1/4 c. light cream

Cut beef in 12 thin slices; pound flat with meat mallet. Season with salt and pepper. Cut pork fat in 12 long strips. Place 1 strip on each beef slice; roll up. Tie each end with string. Saute beef rolls in butter till lightly browned on all sides. Sprinkle with flour; add broth. Cover; simmer for about 1 hour and 30 minutes or till tender, turning occasionally. Add water as needed. Remove strings; place rolls in heated deep serving dish. Skim excess fat from pan drippings. Add cream to drippings; bring just to boiling point. Pour over beef rolls. Serve with boiled potatoes and hot or cold pickled beets. Yield: 6 servings.

Janet Beighle
The Cleveland Plain Dealer

TENDERLOIN OF BEEF IN BURGUNDY ASPIC

2 lb. rare roast tenderloin
   of beef
1/2 c. julienne green peppers
1 c. julienne fresh mushrooms
Lemon juice
3 envelopes unflavored gelatin
1 c. warm water
Black stuffed olives, sliced
Hard-cooked eggs, sliced
1/4 c. julienne dill pickles
1/2 c. julienne pimentos
2 tbsp. lemon juice
1 c. Burgundy
1/2 c. port
1 tbsp. monosodium glutamate
Salt and pepper to taste
4 c. strong clear essence of beef

Cut cooked beef tenderloin into julienne strips. Poach green peppers and mushrooms in a small amount of lemon juice and water. Dissolve gelatin in warm water. Decorate bottoms of individual molds with olives and egg slices. Mix tenderloin, dill pickles, green peppers, pimentos and mushrooms together. Spoon into molds, filling each about 3/4 full. Combine gelatin, 2 tablespoons lemon juice, wines, monosodium glutamate, salt, pepper and essence of beef; pour into molds. Chill in refrigerator overnight. Yield: 8 servings.

Grace Hartley
The Atlanta Journal

GIRARD'S STEAK DIANE

1 tbsp. shallots or green onions
1 tbsp. butter
Freshly ground pepper
3 tbsp. sliced mushrooms
1 tsp. chopped parsley
3 tbsp. (about) dry sherry
1/2 tsp. dry mustard
1 1/2 tbsp. (about) cognac
3 tbsp. beef broth
3 tbsp. whipping cream
1 serving-sized piece thin
   sirloin steak
Butter
Salt

Chop white part of shallots fine. Melt 1 tablespoon butter in skillet; add shallots and a dash of pepper. Cook very slowly for about 10 minutes. Add mushrooms and parsley; cook slowly for 5 minutes longer. Add sherry; cook for 5 more minutes. Stir in mustard. Pour cognac in ladle. Heat till cognac flames; pour into skillet. Add beef broth when flame goes out; bring to a boil. Stir in cream; let bubble till thickness of gravy. Flatten sirloin steak with mallet; grind pepper over steak. Brown quickly on both sides in butter in second skillet; salt to taste. Top with cream sauce. Yield: 1 serving.

Janet Beighle
The Cleveland Plain Dealer

FONDUE BOURGUIGNON

*Beef fillet, club or New York
   steaks*
*Peanut oil or half cooking oil
   and half butter*
Bearnaise Sauce
Curry Sauce
Caper Sauce
Bordelaise Sauce

Trim fillet; cut into 1-inch chunks. Heat peanut oil on kitchen stove; pour into fondue or chafing dish until half full. Heat to about 375 degrees. Place beef chunks on fondue forks; cook in hot oil. Dip into desired sauce to eat.

BEARNAISE SAUCE

3 egg yolks
3/4 tsp. dried tarragon
1 tbsp. tarragon vinegar
1 tsp. lemon juice
1/4 tsp. salt
Dash of cayenne pepper
1/2 c. butter
1 tbsp. chopped parsley

Combine egg yolks, dried tarragon, vinegar, lemon juice, salt and cayenne pepper in blender container; blend for about 30 seconds. Melt butter; heat until foaming but not browned. Turn

blender to high speed. Pour in butter slowly; blend until well mixed. Turn off blender; stir in parsley. Serve at once. Yield: About 1 cup sauce.

CURRY SAUCE

2 tbsp. finely chopped onion
2 tbsp. finely chopped celery
2 tbsp. butter
1/2 tsp. curry powder
2 1/2 tsp. cornstarch
3/4 c. canned bouillon

Cook onion and celery in butter until soft but not browned. Add curry powder and cornstarch; stir in bouillon. Cook, stirring, until mixture boils thoroughly and thickens. Yield: About 1 cup sauce.

CAPER SAUCE

1/2 c. mayonnaise
2 tbsp. chopped drained capers
2 tbsp. chopped parsley
1 tsp. vinegar from capers

Combine all ingredients; mix thoroughly. Yield: 2/3 cup sauce.

BORDELAISE SAUCE

2 tbsp. chopped onion
4 tbsp. butter
1/2 bay leaf
1/4 c. dry red table wine
2 tsp. cornstarch
1/2 c. canned bouillon
1 tsp. chopped parsley

Cook onion in 1 tablespoon butter until soft but not brown. Add bay leaf and wine; simmer until wine is reduced to about 2 tablespoons. Combine cornstarch and bouillon; add to wine mixture. Cook, stirring, until sauce boils and thickens slightly; strain. Add remaining butter and parsley; heat until butter is melted. Yield: 2/3 cup sauce.

Jane Benet
The San Francisco Chronicle

New England Boiled Dinner . . . a gift from the Northeast

NEW ENGLAND BOILED DINNER

4 lb. corned beef
1/2 lb. salt pork
3 qt. boiling water
1/2 c. sugar
3 bay leaves
1 clove of garlic
9 potatoes, peeled
3 yellow turnips
3 carrots
8 white onions, peeled
6 scraped parsnips
1 sm. head cabbage
9 sm. beets (opt.)

Wash beef in cold water; soak for 30 minutes, if very salty. Place beef and salt pork in pot with boiling water; add sugar, bay leaves and garlic. Simmer for 3 hours and 30 minutes or until tender. Thirty minutes before completion of cooking, add potatoes. Peel turnips; slice thickly. Add turnips, carrots, onions and parsnips. Core cabbage; cut into 6 wedges. Place in cooking pot. Dip out 2 cups beef cooking liquor; combine with boiling water to cover cabbage. Cook cabbage until just tender. Cook beets separately until tender. Yield: 6 servings.

Janet Christensen
The Boston Herald Traveler

CORNED BEEF IN FOIL

1   3 to 4-lb. corned beef brisket
1/4 c. water
2 tbsp. pickling spice
1 orange, sliced (opt.)
1 onion, sliced
1 celery stalk with leaves
1 carrot, sliced

Soak corned beef in water to cover for 30 minutes. Preheat oven to 300 degrees. Place large sheet of heavy-duty aluminum foil in shallow pan. Remove corned beef from water; pat dry to remove any salt on surface. Place in center of foil; pour 1/4 cup fresh water over corned beef. Sprinkle with pickling spice; arrange orange slices and vegetables over and around beef. Bring long sides of foil up over beef; seal with tight double fold. Seal ends, turning up to seal in liquid. Bake for 4 hours or until tender. Yield: 8 servings.

Janice Okun
The Buffalo Evening News

ENCHILADA PUFF PIES

1 lb. lean ground beef
1 c. chopped onion
2 8-oz. cans tomato sauce
1 2 1/4-oz. can sliced ripe olives
1/4 c. water
1 1/2 tsp. chili powder
1 tsp. salt
1/4 tsp. cinnamon
6 eggs, separated
2 tbsp. flour
1 c. shredded Monterey Jack,
   Cheddar or Swiss cheese
2 c. corn chips, coarsely crushed
Paprika

Brown beef and onion lightly in skillet; pour off fat. Stir in tomato sauce, olives, water, chili powder, 1/2 teaspoon salt and cinnamon; bring to a boil. Keep hot. Beat egg whites until stiff, moist peaks form. Beat egg yolks with same beater until thick and lemon colored; blend in remaining salt and flour. Fold in cheese; fold in egg whites lightly. Cover bottoms of 4 individual baking dishes with corn chips; spoon on beef mixture. Pile egg mixture on meat; sprinkle with paprika. Bake at 350 degrees for 20 minutes or until topping is puffed and golden; serve immediately.

Janet Christensen
The Boston Herald Traveler

WINEBURGERS

2 lb. ground beef
1 1/2 tsp. salt
1/4 tsp. pepper
1 tbsp. grated onion
1 tsp. dried dill
1/3 to 1/2 c. Burgundy or
   other red wine
6 hamburger buns
6 slices tomato
Crumbled blue cheese

Mix beef with salt, pepper, onion and dill; add just enough wine to moisten.

Refrigerate for at least 1 hour to blend flavors. Shape into patties; broil, pan-fry or barbecue, as desired. Toast buns; butter, if desired. Serve Wineburger on toasted bun; top each with tomato slice and 1 teaspoon blue cheese. Yield: 6 servings.

Jeanne Voltz
The Los Angeles Times

ROLLED STUFFED MEAT LOAF

2 c. soft bread cubes
1/2 c. milk
2 lb. ground beef
1/4 c. minced onion
1 tsp. nutmeg
1 tsp. salt
1/2 tsp. pepper
1 egg

Soak bread cubes in milk. Combine with remaining ingredients; mix thoroughly. Pat beef mixture into 8 x 14-inch rectangle on double sheet of aluminum foil.

FILLING

1/2 c. minced celery
1/2 c. mushroom pieces
1/2 c. minced onion
1/2 c. butter
1 c. soft bread cubes
1/2 c. chopped parsley
1/2 c. American blue cheese,
   crumbled

Saute celery, mushrooms and onion in butter. Add remaining ingredients; spread Filling over meat mixture. Roll as for jelly roll, sealing ends well. Wrap in foil securely. Bake at 450 degrees for 30 minutes. Open foil; bake for 15 minutes longer or until brown. May be frozen before baking; if frozen, bake for 15 minutes longer before opening foil. Freeze half of loaf for later use, if desired.

Janet Christensen
The Boston Herald Traveler

VEAL MOUSSE WITH SUPREME SAUCE

2 1/4 c. cooked veal
4 unbeaten egg whites
1/2 tsp. salt
1/4 tsp. white pepper
1/4 tsp. nutmeg
1/2 c. light cream
Supreme Sauce

Veal Mousse with Supreme Sauce

Grind veal with fine blade of meat grinder. Mix veal and egg whites to smooth paste with fork; add seasonings. Add cream gradually. Place in buttered 4-cup mold or 4 custard cups. Set in pan; fill pan with hot water almost to top of mold. Bake at 350 degrees for 25 to 30 minutes for individual cups or for 40 to 45 minutes for large mold. Place aluminum foil over top of mold to prevent browning. Unmold on hot platter; serve with Supreme Sauce. Yield: 4 servings.

SUPREME SAUCE

2 tbsp. butter
2 tbsp. flour
1/4 tsp. salt
Dash of white pepper
1 c. hot chicken broth
1/2 c. hot cream
1 slightly beaten egg yolk

Melt butter; blend in flour, salt and pepper. Add chicken broth and cream gradually; cook and stir until thickened and smooth. Add small amount of sauce to egg yolk; mix. Add to sauce. Heat through; do not boil. Season to taste.

Ruth Ellen Church
The Chicago Tribune

VEAL CUTLET CORDON BLEU

8 individual veal cutlets
Salt and pepper to taste
4 slices Swiss cheese
4 thin slices Westphalian ham
1 egg, beaten
4 tbsp. flour

1/2 c. fine dry bread or
*   cracker crumbs*
3 tbsp. butter
1 tbsp. oil

Preheat oven to 375 degrees. Pound veal with mallet, working in salt and pepper; trim edges. Place 1 slice cheese and 1 slice ham over half the cutlets so that neither cheese nor ham overlaps edges. Brush edges with egg; top each with another cutlet. Pound edges to seal. Roll each in flour. Dip in egg; dip in crumbs. Saute in mixture of butter and oil until well browned; transfer to casserole or roasting pan. Bake for 20 to 35 minutes. Yield: 4 servings.

Martha H. Schoeps
The Baltimore Sunpapers

VEAL SCALLOPINI

1 lb. veal cutlets
Flour seasoned with salt and pepper
1/4 c. margarine
2 c. sliced fresh mushrooms
1/4 c. Marsala or sherry
2 tbsp. chopped parsley

Slice veal cutlets thin; pound. Dredge in seasoned flour. Saute in margarine until golden brown on both sides. Add mushrooms; saute until veal is browned. Add Marsala; simmer for 3 minutes or until veal is tender. Sprinkle with parsley. Yield: 4 servings.

Jane Benet
The San Francisco Chronicle

BEEF LIVER SAUTE

8 slices beef liver, 1/4 in. thick
1 tsp. salt
1/8 tsp. pepper
1/4 tsp. basil
4 tbsp. flour
4 tbsp. bacon drippings
2 tbsp. butter or margarine
3 tbsp. vermouth or vinegar
Chopped parsley

Remove skin and tough tissue from liver with sharp knife. Coat each slice with seasoned flour. Heat bacon drippings and butter in heavy skillet. Add liver. Cook until brown, piercing liver with fork until no liquid appears on surface. Turn and brown other side, piercing again. Remove to hot platter. Stir vermouth into pan juices; pour over liver. Sprinkle with parsley; serve. Yield: 4 servings.

Alice Petersen
The New York News

Baked Lamb Chops with Fruit
. . . easy and elegant

OVEN-FRIED LIVER

2 lb. sliced veal or calf liver
1 c. corn flake crumbs
1/2 tsp. salt
1/8 tsp. pepper
1/2 c. butter, melted
2 8-oz. pkg. frozen French-
    fried onion rings
1/4 tsp. crushed marjoram
4 strips bacon, diced

Cut liver into serving-sized pieces. Mix corn flake crumbs, salt and pepper together. Dip liver pieces in melted butter; roll in seasoned crumbs. Arrange liver slices and onion rings in single layer on baking sheet lined with foil. Sprinkle onion rings with marjoram; sprinkle liver slices with diced bacon. Bake in preheated 425-degree oven for 10 to 15 minutes or until onions are crisp and liver slices are brown. Yield: 6 servings.

Carol Voshall
The Phoenix Gazette

BAKED LAMB CHOPS WITH FRUIT

6 3/4-in. thick shoulder
    lamb chops
1 1/2 tsp. salt
1/4 tsp. pepper
1/2 c. brown sugar
1 tsp. dry mustard
1/2 c. red table wine
6 pineapple slices
6 thick orange slices
Curly endive or watercress

Season chops on both sides with salt and pepper; place in shallow pan. Mix brown sugar, mustard and wine. Spoon half the sauce over chops. Bake at 400 degrees for about 20 minutes. Turn chops; top each with pineapple and orange slices. Spoon remaining sauce over chops. Bake for 20 minutes longer or until done. Garnish platter with endive. Yield: 6 servings.

Ruth Ellen Church
The Chicago Tribune

ROAST LEG OF LAMB

1   5 to 6-lb. leg of lamb
1 clove of garlic, slivered
1 tbsp. salt
1 tsp. dry mustard
1 c. strong black coffee
2 tsp. sugar
1 c. heavy cream
1/2 c. brandy
2 tbsp. water
5 tbsp. flour
2 tbsp. currant jelly

Preheat oven to 350 degrees. Wipe lamb with damp cloth; make slits with sharp knife. Insert garlic into slits. Blend salt and mustard; rub over lamb. Place on rack in shallow roasting pan. Bake for 1 hour and 30 minutes. Blend coffee, sugar, 2 tablespoons cream, brandy and water in small bowl; baste lamb. Roast for 1 hour and 30 minutes for well done, or until done to taste, basting frequently with coffee mixture. Place lamb on serving dish in warm place. Remove rack. Mix flour and remaining cream to smooth paste in small bowl; stir into pan juices. Cook over low heat, stirring constantly, until thickened and smooth. Add currant jelly; simmer for 2 minutes. Serve with lamb. Yield: 8 servings.

Patricia Williams
The Cincinnati Enquirer

BLUE COAT CHOWDER

2 envelopes instant potato
    soup mix
1   12-oz. can peas
1   8-oz. can tomatoes
1   12-oz. can corn
1 tbsp. butter
2 c. diced cooked ham
1/4 tsp. pepper
2 med. potatoes, sliced
1 med. onion, sliced

Prepare potato soup according to package directions; add peas, toma-toes, corn, butter, ham and pepper. Simmer for 45 minutes. Add potatoes and onion; cook until just tender.

Winifred Phillips
The Baltimore Sun

LUAU PORK AMBROSIA

1   5-lb. pork roast
4 jars baby food strained apricots
1/3 c. honey
1/4 c. fresh lemon juice
1/4 c. soy sauce
1/2 clove of garlic, minced
1 sm. onion, minced
1 c. ginger ale
1/8 tsp. ginger
1/8 tsp. pepper
1   1-lb. 13-oz. can whole
    unpeeled apricots
1 tbsp. grated lemon rind
1/4 c. freshly grated coconut
Parsley sprigs

Remove chine bone from roast; tie roast. Place roast in marinating dish. Combine 2 jars strained apricots, honey, lemon juice, soy sauce, garlic, onion, ginger ale, ginger and pepper; pour over pork. Marinate for 4 to 5 hours, turning occasionally. Line grill with quilted aluminum foil; let coals burn down until covered with gray ash. Remove pork from marinade; reserve marinade. Place roast on spit; cook over low coals for about 3 hours. Cook for 25 minutes longer, basting frequently with marinade. Spread 1 jar strained apricots over roast. Cook for 5 minutes longer. Heat reserved marinade with remaining strained apricots; serve as sauce over roast. Heat whole apricots and lemon rind together. Remove roast to hot serving platter. Garnish with whole apricots; sprinkle with coconut and parsley. Recipe was first prize winner in late Kaiser Cook-Out of 1964. Yield: 6 servings.

Jane Benet
The San Francisco Chronicle

CLEO JOHNS' PORK CROWN ROAST WITH CRANBERRIES

4 c. bread cubes
2 tbsp. grated onion
1 garlic clove, minced
1/2 c. butter
1 1/2 c. fresh cranberries, chopped
1/2 c. dry white wine
1/4 c. sugar
1/2 tsp. marjoram
1/4 tsp. thyme
1 tsp. salt
Freshly ground pepper
1   7-lb. pork crown roast

Saute bread cubes, onion and garlic in butter for 10 minutes. Add cranberries and remaining ingredients except roast. Fill center of roast with mixture. Roast in slow 325-degree oven for 3 hours and 30 minutes or until meat thermometer registers 185 degrees. Mrs. Cleo Johns is a very successful caterer. She started her career picking cotton on her family's farm in North Carolina. She now prepares food for elegant parties in Manhattan and New Jersey. Yield: 6 servings.

Joan Babbage
The Newark Evening News

BAKED PORK CHOPS WITH DRESSING

6 loin pork chops
2 tbsp. flour
1 1/2 tsp. salt
1/4 tsp. pepper
2 tbsp. drippings
Dressing

Have pork chops cut 1 inch thick. Mix flour, salt and pepper; dredge chops in seasoned flour. Brown in drippings. Stand chops in 9 x 5 x 3-inch loaf pan; distribute Dressing evenly between chops. Insert 2 metal skewers, one in each end, to keep loaf together; handles may extend beyond sides of pan. Cover loaf with aluminum foil. Bake at

350 degrees for 45 minutes. Uncover; bake for 15 minutes longer. Let stand in pan for 5 minutes. Remove from pan, lifting carefully, using skewers. Let stand for several minutes. Remove skewers gently so chops do not separate. Yield: 6 servings.

DRESSING

4 c. 1 1/2-in. bread cubes
1 tbsp. grated onion
1/2 c. minced celery
1/4 c. melted butter
1 tsp. each salt and sage

Combine all ingredients; mix lightly.

Elaine Tait
The Philadelphia Inquirer

SWEET AND SOUR PORK CHOPS

4 to 6 loin pork chops
1/3 c. molasses
1/3 c. vinegar
1/2 tsp. salt
1/4 tsp. ginger
1/2 tsp. soy sauce
1   8 1/4-oz. can sliced pineapple
1 tbsp. cornstarch
2 fresh oranges, peeled and
  sectioned
1 green pepper, cut into short strips
1/4 c. halved maraschino
  cherries (opt.)

Have pork chops cut 1 inch thick; trim off excess fat. Heat fat in skillet over medium heat; remove fat from skillet. Brown chops for 5 to 8 minutes on each side; pour off excess fat. Combine molasses, vinegar, salt, ginger and soy sauce. Pour over chops; cover. Simmer for 35 minutes. Remove chops from skillet. Drain pineapple; reserve syrup. Cut pineapple into chunks. Blend cornstarch and 1 tablespoon reserved pineapple syrup; stir into skillet with pineapple, remaining reserved syrup, orange sections, green pepper and cherries. Bring to a boil. Return chops to skillet; cover. Simmer for 5 to 10 minutes longer or until chops are fork-tender and peppers are cooked. Serve with rice, if desired. Yield: 4-6 servings.

Janet Christensen
The Boston Herald Traveler

PORK CHOPS WITH ORANGES AND RAISINS

4 thick pork loin chops
Salt and pepper
1   11-oz. can mandarin
* oranges, drained*
2 tbsp. cornstarch
2 tbsp. sugar
1/8 tsp. allspice
1 1/4 c. hot water
1/4 c. orange curacao
1/4 c. raisins

Trim chops and render fat. Brown chops on both sides in fat; sprinkle with salt and pepper. Place 2 orange sections on each chop. Mix cornstarch, sugar and allspice in saucepan; gradually stir in hot water. Cook and stir until thickened. Add orange curacao and raisins. Pour over chops. Cover; simmer for 1 hour. Serve chops with sauce. Yield: 4 servings.

Ruth Ellen Church
The Chicago Tribune

FIG-STUFFED SPARERIBS

4 to 5 lb. spareribs
Salt
Pepper
2 c. diced tart apples
1 c. diced California dried figs
1/4 c. diced onions
1/4 c. brown sugar
1 tsp. cinnamon
1/2 c. chicken broth or bouillon

Cut spareribs into 2 strips; sprinkle with salt and pepper. Place 1 strip in baking pan. Combine apples, figs, onions, sugar and cinnamon; spread over ribs. Pour broth over apple mixture; top with remaining ribs. Hold together with skewers, if necessary; cover with lid or aluminum foil. Bake at 350 degrees for 1 hour and 30 minutes or until ribs are done. Yield: 6 servings.

Carol Voshall
The Phoenix Gazette

Pork Chops with Oranges and Raisins

BARBECUED SPARERIBS

3 lb. spareribs
1/3 c. hot water
2/3 c. vinegar
1/4 c. butter or margarine
1/3 c. catsup
3 tbsp. horseradish
3 tbsp. Worcestershire sauce
1 tsp. salt
Pepper

Crack spareribs; arrange, meaty side up, in shallow baking pan. Bake in 400-degree oven for 15 minutes; reduce heat to 300 degrees. Mix remaining ingredients for sauce. Bake spareribs for 1 hour longer, turning and basting frequently with sauce, until ribs are brown and crisp. Yield: 6 servings.

Grace Hartley
The Atlanta Journal

HONEY-SHERRY-GLAZED SPARERIBS

    1 8-oz. can tomato sauce
    2 tbsp. wine vinegar
    2 tbsp. minced onion
    Salt and pepper to taste
    1/2 c. honey
    1 clove of garlic, minced
    1 tsp. Worcestershire sauce
    1 tsp. celery seed
    1/2 c. dry sherry
    4 lb. meaty spareribs

Combine tomato sauce, vinegar, onion, salt, pepper, honey, garlic, Worcestershire sauce, celery seed and sherry; simmer for about 20 minutes. Cut ribs into serving pieces. Cook over charcoal for about 30 minutes to cook out fat; pour off drippings. Cook for about 2 hours longer, basting frequently with sauce. May be baked at 400 degrees for 30 minutes. Pour off drippings. Reduce oven temperature to 350 degrees; bake for 1 hour longer, basting frequently with sauce. Yield: 4-6 servings.

Julie Benell
The Dallas Morning News

ENGLISH SAUSAGE ROLLS

    1 1/2 c. flour
    3/4 tsp. salt
    1/2 c. shortening
    3 tbsp. ice water
    1 lb. bulk sausage
    1/2 tsp. salt
    Pepper to taste
    2 tbsp. chopped onion
    1 egg, beaten

Sift flour and 3/4 teaspoon salt together. Cut in shortening; add water. Set pastry aside. Combine remaining ingredients except egg in frying pan. Cook until partially done; drain off excess fat. Chill. Roll pastry into 3 x 30-inch rectangle; place sausage mixture along center of pastry strip. Fold pastry over lengthwise; seal edge. Cut into 3-inch lengths; cut 3 slashes on each. Brush with egg. Bake at 425 degrees for 20 minutes. Yield: 10 rolls.

Jo Ann Vachule
The Fort Worth Star-Telegram

CHICKEN LIVER CASSEROLE

    1 med. onion
    2 cloves of garlic
    1 sm. bunch parsley
    1/2 lb. chicken livers
    3/4 lb. ground chuck
    2 tbsp. olive oil
    2 c. tomato sauce
    1 c. dry red wine
    1 tsp. dried sage
    Pinch of thyme
    Salt and pepper to taste
    1 lb. spaghetti
    Romano or Parmesan cheese

Wash and finely chop onion, garlic and parsley; add to livers and ground chuck. Brown in olive oil in skillet. Pour tomato sauce and wine over skillet mixture. Stir in seasonings; cover. Simmer until sauce is reduced. Cook spaghetti according to package directions until almost done; drain. Mix with 3/4 of the chicken liver sauce. Pour into a greased 1 1/2-quart casserole. Grate enough cheese to sprinkle over top of casserole; pour remaining sauce over cheese. Bake, uncovered, in 300-degree oven for about 30 minutes or until bubbly. Simple green salad or an assortment of relishes are best with this dish. Yield: 4 servings.

Helen Civelli Brown
The San Francisco Examiner

VEAL AND SWEETBREADS HAWAIIAN

    2 sweetbreads
    2 tbsp. butter
    2 tbsp. flour

1 3/4 c. milk, heated
1/4 c. cream
1 egg yolk
2 tbsp. dry sherry
1 c. cooked veal, diced
1/2 c. diced pineapple
Salt and pepper
1/2 c. sliced cooked mushrooms

Soak and parboil sweetbreads; cool and dice. Melt butter in saucepan. Mix in flour; add milk. Cook sauce over low heat for at least 30 minutes. Combine cream and egg yolk; stir into sauce. Add sherry, veal and pineapple; stir gently. Season to taste. Fold in sweetbreads and mushrooms carefully. Serve in patty shells, over rice or on toast. Served by Mrs. Lyndon B. Johnson at a White House buffet for the press.

Elinor Lee
The Washington Post

PERDICES DE CAPELLAN

4 slices boiled ham, halved
8 thin slices veal
1/2 lb. fresh pork sausage
3 tbsp. butter
2 tbsp. flour
1 clove of garlic, crushed
1 tsp. salt
1/4 tsp. each pepper, cinnamon and
    caraway seed
1/3 c. dry white wine
1 c. stock or bouillon
1/4 c. chopped parsley
1/3 c. chopped pimento-stuffed
    olives

Place 1/2 slice ham on each veal slice; spread sausage over ham. Roll up jelly roll fashion; fasten with picks. Melt butter. Add veal roll-ups; cook over low heat until browned on all sides. Remove veal rolls; reserve drippings. Blend flour, garlic, salt, pepper, cinnamon and caraway seed into reserved drippings; add wine and stock gradu-ally. Cook over low heat, stirring constantly, until thickened. Add veal rolls, parsley and olives; mix well. Cover; cook over low heat for 30 minutes, stirring occasionally. May be served with steamed rice. Name of this rich entree, which comes from northern Spain, means Chaplain's Partridges, although there are no partridges in ingredients. A Spanish version, no doubt, of our stuffed veal birds. Yield: 8 servings.

Helen Civelli Brown
The San Francisco Examiner

VENISON STEAK

2 lb. venison steak
1 onion, chopped
1 leek, chopped
3 oz. butter
1 stalk celery, chopped
2 carrots, chopped
1/2 tbsp. meat extract or 1
    bouillon cube
2 tbsp. flour
1/2 bottle white wine
Sugar, salt and pepper to taste
1 oz. truffles or mushrooms (opt.)
4 slices bread

Pound venison lightly. Skin and wash venison; cut into thick steaks. Saute onion and leek in butter. Add celery, carrots and about 2 cups boiling water. Bring to a boil; add meat extract. Cook until stock is well flavored. Thicken stock with flour; add wine, sugar, salt and pepper. Rub stock through fine sieve. Dip venison steaks into stock; fry on both sides until tender. Add truffles. Remove crusts from bread; cut into triangles. Fry until crisp. Arrange steaks on hot plate; cover with remaining stock. Garnish with bread triangles. Serve with glazed chestnuts or sauteed small mashed potato balls.

Bertha Scott
The Indianapolis News

Chicken Favorites plus Recipes for Turkey, Duck, Cornish Hens and Game Birds

C hicken on Sunday used to be considered a sign of wealth in this country. An American presidential candidate — Herbert Hoover — ran on the slogan, "A Chicken in Every Pot."

Chicken, turkey, duck, and goose have always been favorite fare in America, and in the past were usually served only on holidays or other special occasions. Today, with new breeding, raising, and preserving techniques, they are not only always available but are also low in price.

Americans have had long experience in cooking fowl, going back to the turkey served at the first Thanksgiving in Plymouth, Massachusetts. Out of this long history has come a collection of great recipes for cooking poultry and other fowl. The best of these recipes have been selected by America's leading newspaper food editors and are presented here. Among them you will find Country Captain, Chicken Antonio, Stuffed Squab, Savory Wild Duck and Pheasant in Wine.

BRUNSWICK STEW

1 hen
4 cans tomatoes
1 can green peas
1 can mushrooms
1 qt. sliced okra
1/2 lb. butter
8 ears of corn, cut from cob
5 potatoes, cubed
3 onions, chopped
Juice of 1 lemon
Pepper, salt and Worcestershire
   sauce to taste

Boil hen until tender; reserve stock. Remove bones; grind chicken. Mix reserved stock, chicken and remaining ingredients. Cook over low heat for about 6 hours, stirring frequently, being careful not to let stew burn.

Jean Thwaite
The Atlanta Constitution

VIVA LA CHICKEN

4 whole chicken breasts
1 doz. corn tortillas
1 can cream of chicken soup
1 can mushroom soup
1 c. milk
1 onion, grated
1 to 1 1/2 5-oz. cans green
   chile salsa
1 lb. Cheddar cheese, shredded

Wrap chicken breasts in aluminum foil. Bake at 400 degrees for 1 hour or until tender. Remove bone; cut chicken into large pieces. Reserve chicken broth. Cut tortillas into 1-inch strips or squares. Mix soups, milk, onion and salsa. Pour 1 or 2 spoonfuls reserved chicken broth or water in greased large shallow baking dish. Place layer of tortillas in broth; add layer of chicken. Add layer of soup mixture. Repeat layers until all ingredients are used, ending with soup mixture. Sprinkle cheese over top. Refrigerate for 24

hours to allow flavors to blend. Bake at 300 degrees for 1 hour to 1 hour and 30 minutes. Yield: 8 servings.

Jeanne Voltz
The Los Angeles Times

BAKED CHICKEN BREASTS

10 chicken breasts
Salt
2 c. sour cream
1 tbsp. Worcestershire sauce
1/2 tsp. red hot sauce
1 clove of garlic
2 tsp. salt
1 tsp. paprika
Fine dry bread crumbs
Butter

Have butcher bone chicken breasts. Wipe with damp cloth; salt lightly. Place in shallow dish. Mix sour cream with seasonings; pour over chicken. Turn each chicken breast until well coated. Cover; refrigerate overnight. Wipe off excess sour cream mixture; roll each c h i c k e n breast in bread crumbs. Roll each breast into individual serving; place in baking dish. Chill for 1 hour and 30 minutes. Place small amount of butter on each serving. Bake, covered, at 325 degrees for 30 minutes. Uncover; bake for 1 hour longer. Yield: 10 servings.

Mary Hart
The Minneapolis Tribune

CHICKEN JERUSALEM

6 chicken breasts
2 tsp. salt
1/4 tsp. pepper
1/2 tsp. paprika
3/4 c. flour
6 tbsp. butter or margarine
1/2 lb. fresh mushrooms, sliced
2 chicken bouillon cubes or 2 tsp.
   instant chicken bouillon
2 c. boiling water

1/2 c. sherry
1/2 c. evaporated milk
1/2 tsp. dried rosemary
1 No. 303 can artichoke
 hearts, drained

Place chicken breasts, two at a time, in paper bag with salt, pepper, paprika and 1/2 cup flour. Shake to coat each piece thoroughly. Reserve remaining flour mixture. Brown chicken in butter; remove to 3-quart casserole. Add mushrooms to frying pan, adding more butter if needed. Cook gently until mushrooms are golden, about 10 minutes. Sprinkle reserved flour mixture and 4 tablespoons flour over mushrooms; slowly stir in combined bouillon, liquids and rosemary. Cook over moderate heat, stirring constantly, until thickened. Arrange artichoke hearts in between chicken pieces in casserole. Pour hot mushroom sauce over top; cover. Bake at 350 degrees for 45 minutes. Yield: 6 servings.

Margaret C. Bowers
The Oakland Tribune

CANNELLONI ALLA NERONE

3 whole chicken breasts
1 c. butter
1/2 lb. chicken livers
1/2 lb. prosciutto or Virginia ham
1/2 c. (about) flour
2 c. milk
2 c. cream
2 tsp. salt
Pepper to taste
3 doz. Crepes
2 c. grated Parmesan cheese

Saute chicken breasts in 1/2 cup butter until brown and tender; remove from bone. Cook livers in same butter for 2 to 3 minutes. Grind chicken with livers and ham. Melt remaining butter; blend in flour. Add milk and cream. Add salt and pepper. Mix small amount of sauce with chicken-ham

mixture to make spreadable blend; taste for seasoning. Spread chicken-ham mixture in center of each Crepe, leaving small margin; roll tight. Place filled pancakes side by side in shallow baking dish in one layer; spread with cheese. Pour remaining sauce over cheese. Bake at 375 degrees for 25 minutes or until hot and browned. Yield: 12 servings.

CREPES

2 c. sifted flour
1/2 tsp. salt
4 eggs, beaten
3 c. milk
2 tbsp. melted butter

Beat flour, salt, eggs, milk and butter until smooth; let stand for 1 hour. Bake paper-thin pancakes on greased griddle or in 6 or 7-inch omelet pan. May use favorite pancake recipe instead of Crepes recipe, if desired. Dish may be prepared and refrigerated before baking; recipe is my own adaptation of an Italian specialty and appears in my book, "Pancakes Aplenty".

Ruth Ellen Church
The Chicago Tribune

Cannelloni Alla Nerone
. . . rich crepes filled with poultry

FRECKLED DRUMSTICKS

1/2 c. margarine
1 c. fine bread crumbs
1/2 c. finely chopped peanuts
1 tsp. grated orange rind
1 tsp. salt
1/4 tsp. pepper
8 broiler-fryer chicken drumsticks
1/4 c. orange juice
2 tbsp. soy sauce

Melt margarine in foil-lined 14 x 10 x 2-inch baking pan. Combine bread crumbs, peanuts, orange rind, salt and pepper. Roll drumsticks in melted margarine then in crumb mixture; place drumsticks in remaining margarine in pan. Bake, uncovered, in 375-degree oven for 30 minutes. Mix orange juice and soy sauce together. Spoon 1/2 of the mixture over drumsticks; bake for 15 more minutes. Turn drumsticks; spoon on remaining juice mixture. Bake for 15 minutes longer or until brown and tender. Yield: 4 servings.

Winifred Phillips
The Baltimore Sun

LEMON-BARBECUED CHICKEN

2 2 1/2 to 3-lb. broiling chickens
1 c. salad oil
1/2 c. fresh lemon juice
1 tbsp. salt
1 tsp. paprika
2 tsp. onion powder
2 tsp. sweet basil, crushed
1/2 tsp. thyme, crushed
1/2 tsp. garlic powder

Split chickens; clean well. Place in shallow glass dish. Combine oil, lemon juice, salt, paprika, onion powder, basil, thyme and garlic powder in pint jar; shake well to blend. Pour over chickens; cover tightly. Marinate for 6 to 8 hours or overnight, turning occasionally. Remove to room temperature about 1 hour before ready to grill. Place chickens on grill, skin side up; cook for 20 to 25 minutes, basting frequently with marinade. Turn chickens; repeat basting until chickens are golden brown and cooked through, about 20 minutes longer. Chickens may be placed about 8 inches from broiler heat and broiled in oven, if desired. Yield: 4 servings.

Ann M. Criswell
The Houston Chronicle

ROASTED CHICKEN CALABRIAN

2 2 1/2 to 3-lb. frying chickens
Olive oil
1 tsp. dried oregano, crumbled
2 cloves of garlic, minced
Salt
1 c. light muscat, sauterne
or other white wine
Juice of 1 lemon
1 1-lb. 1-oz. can Kodota
figs, drained
1 med. thin skinned orange
California sherry

Quarter and brush chickens with oil. Sprinkle with seasonings. Place in shallow baking pan, skin side up. Bake, uncovered, in 400-degree oven for 20 to 25 minutes or until brown. Combine wine and lemon juice; baste chickens frequently during baking. Prick figs with fork; slice orange 1/4 inch thick. Marinate figs and orange slices in sherry. Turn chickens; brown for 15 to 20 minutes. Taste; add more salt if needed. Add figs and orange slices; continue baking for 5 to 10 minutes or until golden. Finish basting with sherry marinade if chickens seem dry. Yield: 8 servings.

Margaret C. Bowers
The Oakland Tribune

COUNTRY CAPTAIN

1 3 1/2 to 4-lb. young tender hen
Flour
Salt
Pepper
Lard
2 onions, finely chopped
2 green peppers, finely chopped
1 sm. clove of garlic
1/2 tsp. white pepper
2 tsp. (rounded) curry powder
   or to taste
2 No. 303 cans tomatoes
1/2 tsp. chopped parsley
1/2 tsp. powdered thyme
2 c. cooked rice, drained
3 tbsp. (rounded) currants
1/4 lb. roasted almonds

Country Captain

Cut hen into serving pieces; remove skin. Roll in mixture of flour, salt and pepper; fry in lard in skillet. Remove chicken from skillet; keep hot. Add onions, green peppers and garlic to lard in skillet; cook over low heat, stirring constantly, until tender. Add salt to taste, white pepper, curry powder, tomatoes, parsley and thyme. Place chicken in roaster; pour tomato mixture over chicken. Rinse skillet with water; pour over chicken to cover. Cover with lid. Bake at 350 degrees for about 45 minutes or until chicken is tender. Place chicken on platter; place rice around chicken. Add currants to tomato mixture; pour over rice. Sprinkle almonds over top; garnish with parsley. Secret of dish's success is in keeping chicken hot after browning. Yield: 6-8 servings.

Jean Thwaite
The Atlanta Constitution

POT O' GOLD CHICKEN CURRY

1 1/2 c. quick-cooking rice
1/4 c. dried currants
3/4 tsp. salt
1 1/2 c. water
1/3 c. sherry
2 tbsp. butter
1 tbsp. flour
1 c. milk
2 tsp. (or more) curry powder
1 1/2 c. diced chicken or turkey
Salt and pepper to taste

Combine rice, currants, 3/4 teaspoon salt, water and wine in saucepan. Bring to a boil; cover. Remove from heat; let stand for 10 minutes. Add butter. Combine flour with 1/4 cup milk in large saucepan. Mix well. Cook and stir, adding remaining milk with curry powder gradually, till mixture thickens. Add chicken; season with salt and pepper to taste. Heat over low flame, stirring occasionally. Serve with hot rice. Curry is usually served with variety of condiments such as chutney, coconut, slivered almonds, chopped dates, white raisins, sliced oranges and bananas. Place separately in small serving dishes. To serve rice in molded shape, let rice and currants stand in pan for 5 minutes, rather than 10. Press into ring mold or mixing bowl; let stand for 5 minutes. Place serving dish on top of mold; invert and lift off mold. Serve chicken curry in center of ring. Shrimp or crab meat may be used if desired. Yield: 4 servings.

Janet Christensen
The Boston Herald Traveler

WINE HERB-BAKED CHICKEN

1 broiler-fryer, cut up
1/4 c. dry vermouth
1/4 c. lemon juice
1/4 c. minced parsley
1 clove of garlic, crushed
3 tsp. salt
1/2 tsp. grated lemon peel
1/2 tsp. pepper
1/4 tsp. each rubbed sage and
*   thyme leaves*
1/2 c. flour
1/3 c. shortening

Place chicken in large bowl. Combine vermouth, lemon juice, parsley, garlic, 1 teaspoon salt, lemon peel, 1/4 teaspoon pepper, sage and thyme. Pour over chicken. Cover; marinate for several hours or overnight, turning occasionally. Drain marinade from chicken; reserve. Shake chicken in paper bag containing flour and remaining salt and pepper. Brown chicken in shortening in large skillet. Remove chicken; place in shallow baking dish. Pour reserved marinade over chicken. Bake, uncovered, at 375 degrees for 45 minutes. Yield: 4 servings.

Jeanne Voltz
The Los Angeles Times

Wine Herb-Baked Chicken

SAVORY CHICKEN

2 broiler-fryers, quartered or cut up
Thyme, sage and garlic powder
*   to taste*
Freshly ground pepper to taste
Butter

Arrange chicken pieces, skin side down, in shallow baking pans; season generously. Turn chicken, skin side up; season generously. Bake at 325 degrees for about 1 hour and 15 minutes or until done, basting occasionally with pan drippings. Pour off liquid and drippings; dot or brush with butter. Bake for about 10 minutes longer or until brown.

Dorothee Polson
The Arizona Republic

LEMON CHICKEN

6 to 8 pieces frying chicken
1 whole lemon
1/3 c. flour
1 1/2 tsp. salt
1/2 tsp. paprika
4 tbsp. cooking oil
2 tbsp. brown sugar
1 lemon, thinly sliced
1 c. chicken broth or bouillon
2 sprigs of fresh mint or 1/2 tsp.
*   dried mint (opt.)*

Wash chicken; drain on paper towels. Grate peel of lemon; set aside. Cut lemon; rub chicken pieces with juice. Shake chicken in paper bag with flour, salt and paprika. Brown chicken slowly in oil; arrange in baking pan in single layer. Sprinkle with grated peel and brown sugar; cover with sliced lemon. Pour chicken broth over chicken; place mint on top. Cover. Bake at 375 degrees for 40 to 45 minutes. Remove mint before serving. Lemon slices enhance chicken with subtle accent. Yield: 6-8 servings.

Marjorie Anderson "Mary Cullen"
The Oregon Journal

CHICKEN CACCIATORE

1 chicken
1/2 c. olive oil
1 clove of garlic
1 1/4 tsp. salt
1/4 tsp. pepper
1/2 tbsp. rosemary
6 chopped anchovy fillets
2/3 c. wine vinegar
1 c. Chianti
3 tbsp. tomato paste
1/3 c. chicken bouillon

Cut chicken into serving pieces. Bring oil to high heat; saute chicken and garlic for 5 minutes, turning chicken constantly. Remove garlic. Mix salt, pepper, rosemary, anchovies, wine vinegar and Chianti; add to chicken. Simmer, uncovered, until liquid is reduced one-third. Dissolve tomato paste in chicken bouillon; pour over chicken. Simmer, covered, for 20 minutes.

Beverly Kees
The Minneapolis Star

TONY BARBARA'S CHICKEN ANTONIO

1 3 to 4-lb. chicken, cut up
1 garlic clove
4 slices prosciutto
4 slices salami
1/4 lb. dry sausage (opt.)
1 onion, chopped
1 stalk celery, chopped
1 sm. can tomatoes
2 green peppers, cut in strips

Fry chicken and garlic until brown; remove garlic. Add prosciutto, salami, sausage, onion and celery; fry until lightly browned. Add tomatoes; cook for about 1 hour. Add green peppers; cook until peppers are done.

Joan Babbage
The Newark Evening News

CHICKEN AND RICE SOUP BAKE

3/4 c. rice or brown rice
1 pkg. onion soup mix
1 2 1/2 to 3-lb. cut-up fryer
1 10 1/2-oz. can cream of
*   mushroom soup*
Garlic salt and paprika to taste

Place rice on bottom of baking dish; sprinkle with onion soup mix. Arrange chicken over rice. Mix mushroom soup with enough water to make 2 1/2 cups liquid; pour over chicken. Sprinkle with garlic salt and paprika. Bake at 350 degrees for 1 hour or until chicken is tender. Yield: 4 servings.

Dorothy Neighbors
The Seattle Times

Choice Chicken

CHOICE CHICKEN

> 1   3-lb. chicken, cut up
> Salt and pepper to taste
> 3 tbsp. margarine
> 1 c. diced ham
> 1   10 1/2-oz. can cream
>   of chicken soup
> 1 c. dry white wine or
>   pineapple juice
> 1/2 lb. seedless grapes
>   or 1 c. white raisins

Season chicken with salt and pepper; brown in margarine in heavy skillet. Add ham; brown slightly. Stir in undiluted soup; add wine slowly until well blended. Cook, covered, over low heat for 30 minutes; add water, if necessary. Add grapes; cook for 10 minutes longer. If raisins are used, plump in wine for at least 1 hour. Yield: 4 servings.

> *Verna McCallum*
> *The Indianapolis Star*

CORNISH HENS WITH WILD RICE

> 1 c. wild rice
> 1/2 c. chopped onion
> 1/2 c. chopped celery
> 1/2 c. butter
> 1/2 c. fresh mushrooms
> 1 tsp. salt
> 1/2 tsp. poultry seasoning
> 1/2 tsp. celery salt
> 1/2 tsp. marjoram
> 1/2 tsp. thyme
> 1/4 tsp. freshly ground pepper
> 6   16 to 18-oz. Rock Cornish hens

Cook wild rice according to package directions. Saute onion and celery in butter until tender. Add mushrooms; cook for 2 or 3 minutes longer. Combine with wild rice; add seasonings and mix. Stuff hens loosely with rice mixture; place in roasting pan. Bake, uncovered, in moderate 350-degree oven for about 1 hour to 1 hour and 15 minutes. Baste with additional butter once or twice during baking time. Two tablespoons Marsala wine may be added to the basting butter if desired. Yield: 6 servings.

> *Martha H. Schoeps*
> *The Baltimore Sunpapers*

CORNISH HENS WITH APPLE-PECAN STUFFING

> 4 tbsp. butter
> 6 sm. green onions with
>   1-in. tops, sliced
> 1   3-oz. can chopped mushrooms,
>   drained
> 1/2 c. chopped pecans
> 1 sm. unpeeled apple, chopped
> 6 slices bread, torn into pieces
> Salt and pepper to taste
> Dry vermouth
> 4 Rock Cornish game hens
> Cooking oil
> 8 slices lean bacon, halved

Preheat oven to 350 degrees. Melt butter. Add onions and mushrooms;

saute until onions are transparent. Toss onion m i x t u r e with pecans, apple, bread, salt and pepper. Add enough dry vermouth to hold mixture together. Stuff each hen with mixture. Close cavities with skewers. Brush hens on all sides with cooking oil. Place hens, breast sides up, on rack in roasting pan. Bake for about 2 hours or until done. Arrange bacon on top of hens during last 45 minutes of cooking time. Yield: 4 servings.

Helen Dollaghan
The Denver Post

STUFFED SQUAB

1/4 lb. butter
1 chopped onion
1 chopped celery stalk
6 slices bread
Dash of salt and pepper
6 boned squab
2 c. red wine
1 tbsp. butter
1 tbsp. flour

Combine 1/4 pound butter, onion, celery, bread, salt and pepper; mix well. Form stuffing into 6 egg shapes. Wrap 1 squab around each egg; place in aluminum foil. Bake in 350-degree oven for 1 hour. Pour wine in saucepan; boil until liquid is reduced by half. Melt 1 tablespoon butter in saucepan; stir in flour. Add wine; cook until thick, stirring constantly. Pour over squab; serve with wild rice.

Winifred Phillips
The Baltimore Sun

TURKEY MOUSSE

3 tbsp. butter
3 tbsp. flour
1 c. milk
1/2 tsp. salt
1/4 tsp. pepper
2 c. cooked turkey, finely shredded
1/2 c. soft bread crumbs

2 eggs, slightly beaten
1 can cream of mushroom soup

Prepare white sauce of butter, flour, milk and seasonings; cool slightly. Add turkey, bread crumbs and eggs. Pour into individual greased molds or muffin tins. Set in pan of hot water. Bake in 350-degree oven for 45 minutes or until knife inserted in center comes out clean. Unmold. Heat soup according to can directions. Serve over top. Yield: 8 servings.

Beverly Kees
The Minneapolis Star

TURKEY CREPES

1 tbsp. butter
2 tsp. flour
1/2 c. light cream
Salt and pepper
1 c. chopped leftover turkey
1/4 c. chopped almonds
1/4 c. chopped mushrooms, sauteed
2 c. biscuit mix
1 1/4 c. milk
1 egg
1 tbsp. brown sugar
2 tbsp. salad oil
Sour cream
1/4 c. grated cheese
2 tbsp. butter

Melt 1 tablespoon butter in skillet; blend in flour. Add cream gradually, stirring until sauce is smooth and thickened. Season to taste; simmer for 1 minute. Add turkey, almonds and mushrooms; mix well. Mix biscuit mix, milk, egg, brown sugar and oil; make large pancakes. Place 1 tablespoon turkey mixture in center; roll up. Arrange close together in shallow greased baking pan. Top each with 1 teaspoon sour cream; sprinkle cheese over all. Dot with 2 tablespoons butter. Bake in 375-degree oven for 20 minutes. Yield: 6 servings.

Yvonne Rothert
The Oregonian

ROAST TURKEY IN A PAPER SACK

1 thawed turkey

Preheat oven to 325 degrees. Prepare turkey as for roasting, with stuffing if desired. Slide into large, heavy brown paper sack, without holes. Twist end shut; tie with string. Place on rack in broiler pan. Bake for 25 minutes per pound for 12 pounds or under and for 20 minutes per pound for larger turkeys. Do not peek, poke or baste. Remove broiler pan from oven. Carefully tear sack away, allowing juices to run into drip pan below. Slide turkey onto heated platter. Remove rack; prepare gravy in pan.

Marjean Phillips Busby
The Kansas City Star and Times

SWEET-SOUR DUCKLING

1 4 1/2 to 5-lb. frozen duckling
1 tbsp. cooking oil
1 1-lb. 4 1/2-oz. can sliced
pineapple
1 tbsp. soy sauce
1 clove of garlic, finely minced
1/2 tsp. salt
3/4 tsp. ginger
1/2 c. sugar
2 tbsp. cornstarch
1 c. water
1/3 c. vinegar
1 med. green pepper
1/2 c. 1-in. pieces green onion
Hot cooked rice

Thaw duckling; cut into quarters. Wash, drain and dry duckling quarters. Brown both sides of quarters in oil, turning, as needed, to brown evenly. Drain pineapple slices; reserve syrup. Combine 1/2 cup pineapple syrup, soy sauce, garlic, salt and ginger. Mix well; pour over duckling. Cover; cook slowly for about 1 hour to 1 hour and 15 minutes or until duckling is tender, turning once. Remove duckling from pan; drain off excess fat. Combine sugar, cornstarch, remaining pineapple syrup, water and vinegar. Add to remaining pan drippings. Cook, stirring constantly, until clear and thickened. Reserve 4 pineapple slices for garnishing; cut remaining slices into chunks. Cut green pepper in 1-inch squares; cut onion in 1-inch pieces. Add pineapple chunks, green pepper and green onion to sauce; heat. Serve duckling on rice; top with sauce. Garnish with pineapple slices. Yield: 4 servings.

Cyrilla Riley
The Detroit News

GINGER-ORANGE GLAZED DUCK

1 4 1/2 to 5-lb. frozen duck
1/2 tsp. salt
1 13 1/2-oz. can pineapple chunks
2 tbsp. chopped candied ginger
1/3 c. light corn syrup
1/2 c. sugar
1 tbsp. grated orange rind
1/2 c. orange juice
3 tbsp. lemon juice
1 c. diced orange sections
1 tbsp. cornstarch

Thaw duck; wash, drain and pat dry. Sprinkle neck and body cavity with salt. Tie wings against breast; tie legs together loosely, looping chord around tail. Place on rack in roasting pan. Bake at 325 degrees about 2 hours and 30 minutes or until duck is tender. Drain pineapple; reserve juice. Combine pineapple juice, ginger, syrup, sugar, orange rind, orange juice and lemon juice; brush glaze over duck. Bake for 30 minutes longer, basting 3 or 4 times. Add pineapple chunks and orange sections to remaining glaze; blend in cornstarch. Cook until thickened and clear. Serve with duck. Yield: 4 servings.

Dorothy Neighbors
The Seattle Times

JELLY-WINE SAUCE FOR WILD DUCK

1 c. currant jelly
1 c. red wine
Pinch of powdered ginger
Pinch of powdered cloves
1 tbsp. lemon juice
Game drippings
Flour
1 tbsp. cognac

Melt currant jelly in saucepan over low heat. Add red wine; mix well. Simmer while adding ginger, cloves and lemon juice. Thicken with equal parts strained game drippings and flour, mixed until smooth. Add cognac just before serving. May be served with goose or venison.

Jean Thwaite
The Atlanta Constitution

SAVORY WILD DUCK

Wild ducks
Salt and pepper
Monosodium glutamate
Bacon fat
1/2 c. red wine
1/2 c. consomme
1/2 tsp. (about) sage

Skin and wash ducks thoroughly. Season with salt and pepper; sprinkle with monosodium glutamate. Cover with melted bacon fat; place in baking pan. Bake in 500-degree oven for 20 minutes or until brown. Combine wine, consomme and sage to taste; pour over ducks. Cover tightly. Bake in 225-degree oven for about 2 hours or until tender. Gamy taste can be alleviated by soaking game birds for at least 10 hours in pan of water to which 2 tablespoons salt and 1 tablespoon soda have been added for each gallon of water. Wash well before cooking.

Opal M. Crandall
The San Diego Union

PLEASANT PHEASANT

1 pheasant, cut in serving pieces
Seasoned flour
4 tbsp. butter or margarine
1/2 c. brandy
1 c. dry red wine
3 green onions, including tops
1/2 tsp. thyme
1/2 tbsp. chopped parsley
1 pt. coffee cream

Rinse pheasant under cold water; drain. Coat pieces in seasoned flour. Brown slowly in butter in heavy skillet with tight-fitting lid. Turn frequently. Add warm brandy; ignite, shaking pan until flame dies. Remove pheasant; add wine. Loosen all particles in pan. Add onions, thyme and parsley; blend well. Return pheasant to pan. Cover; cook over low heat for about 45 minutes. Remove pheasant; add coffee cream. Heat; do not boil. Cover pheasant with sauce; serve.

Cyrilla Riley
The Detroit News

PHEASANT IN WINE

2 pheasant, split in half
4 strips bacon
3/4 c. red wine
1 sm. onion, sliced
1/4 tsp. thyme
1 c. sour cream

Brush pheasant with butter; sprinkle with salt and pepper. Brown on each side under broiler. Place skin side up in shallow baking pan; place bacon slice on each. Pour wine over pheasant. Add sliced onion to pan; add thyme. Cover. Bake in 325-degree oven for 30 minutes. Uncover; bake for 30 minutes longer or until tender. Cook giblets until tender. Chop; add to pan juices. Remove pheasant to hot platter; stir sour cream into pan juices. Serve over pheasant. Yield: 4 servings.

Janice Okun
The Buffalo Evening News

Fish and Shellfish Delicacies Bring
the Seas and the Lakes to Your Table

With a great ocean on either side, the Gulf of Mexico to the south, and with lakes and rivers plentifully scattered throughout the land, America has always had a large and varied supply of fish and shellfish. The oceans yield codfish, clams, oysters, halibut, mackerel, and many other popular foods. The lakes and rivers give us trout, bass, pike, salmon and other delicately flavored fish.

From Boston, from New Orleans, from San Francisco, and from other noted centers of fish cookery come seafood recipes chosen by the country's most noted food editors. Whether you catch your own or buy your seafood at a neighborhood market, your cookery can become legendary with this exciting collection of dishes chosen especially to highlight the flavor of fish and shellfish.

Choose from such great recipes as Redfish Courtbouillon, Fish Fillets Florentine, Trout Meuniere, Crayfish Etoaffee, Steamed Mussels, Lobster Cantonese, and Scampi.

57

SILVERGATE FISH STEW

2 lb. halibut or rock cod
2 lge. potatoes, diced
1/4 lb. salt pork, diced
2 lge. onions, chopped
1/2 tsp. sugar
1 can minced clams
1 qt. milk
Salt and pepper to taste
Minced parsley
Paprika

Boil halibut in salted water until tender; remove bones. Flake fish. Boil potatoes in fish broth until tender. Fry salt pork in frying pan until crisp. Remove pork from pan. Add onions; cook until golden. Add sugar; stir. Add fish, potatoes with broth and clams. Add milk slowly; bring to simmer. Season; garnish with parsley and/or paprika. A New England background combined with a touch of the South equals this marvelous fish dish served with Hush Puppies. What a way to sup on a cool evening! Yield: 8 servings.

Kay Jarvis
The San Diego Evening Tribune

BREAKFAST FISH

Oil
1 pkg. frozen fish fillets, thawed
Salt and pepper to taste
Fresh lemon juice to taste
Butter or margarine

Pour small amount of oil in baking pan. Arrange fish in pan, skin side down; season with salt, pepper and lemon juice. Dot or brush with butter. Broil for 8 to 10 minutes without turning; serve with additional lemon juice. This is a fast, economical and extremely nourishing breakfast dish. Yield: 4 servings.

Dorothee Polson
The Arizona Republic

Breakfast Fish ▶

REDFISH COURTBOUILLON

1   4 to 6-lb. redfish
1/2 c. salad oil
1 c. flour
1 c. minced onions
2 1/2 c. canned tomatoes
2 bay leaves
1/2 c. chopped green pepper
2 tbsp. minced garlic
4 tbsp. minced parsley
Salt and pepper to taste
1 glass claret wine (opt.)
1/2 lemon, thinly sliced

Slice redfish across backbone in slices, 3 inches wide. Prepare golden brown roux with oil, flour and onions. Add tomatoes; simmer until thickened. Add redfish; cook for about 10 minutes. Add remaining ingredients except wine and lemon; add water to make thick gravy. Simmer until fish is nearly done. Add wine and lemon slices; simmer for 5 minutes. It should be noted that this mixture should simmer and never boil.

Rachel Daniel
The New Orleans Times-Picayune

FISH STEAKS SEVILLE

1/2 c. chopped green pepper
1/4 c. chopped onion
1 clove of garlic, minced
3 tbsp. butter
1   1-lb. can tomatoes
2 tsp. chili powder
1/2 tsp. salt
1/4 tsp. pepper
1 bay leaf
1 tsp. cornstarch
1 tbsp. water
2 lb. fresh or frozen halibut
  or salmon steaks

Saute green pepper, onion and garlic in butter until wilted. Add tomatoes, chili powder, salt, pepper and bay leaf; simmer for 5 minutes. Blend cornstarch with water; stir into hot tomato sauce. Cook, stirring, until thickened. Arrange halibut steaks in single layer in well-greased baking pan; pour sauce over all. Bake at 350 degrees for 30 minutes or until fish flakes easily when tested with fork. Remove fish from pan carefully with pancake turner. Serve with French fries. Sauce may be varied by adding 1 teaspoon oregano, basil or other herb and omitting chili powder. Yield: 4-6 servings.

Marian O'Brien
The St. Louis Globe-Democrat

FISH FILLETS FLORENTINE

2   9-oz. pkg. frozen or 1 lb.
  fresh spinach
9 tbsp. butter
2 lb. frozen sole, thawed, or
  fresh flounder fillets
1 c. dry white wine or water
1 tsp. salt
1 1/2 tbsp. flour
1 c. grated Swiss cheese
1 c. heavy cream

Cook spinach according to package directions; drain well. Melt 2

Fish Fillets Florentine

tablespoons butter in saucepan; saute spinach over low heat for 2 to 3 minutes. Place spinach in center of heatproof serving dish; keep warm. Grease 12-inch skillet with 2 tablespoons butter. Fold fillets in half or thirds; place in pan. Add wine to just cover fillets; add salt. Cover; simmer for 2 to 3 minutes. Remove fillets; arrange around spinach in serving dish. Keep warm. Blend flour and 1 tablespoon butter. Boil liquid in skillet until reduced by half; add flour mixture, a small amount at a time, stirring until sauce is smooth. Reserve 3 tablespoons cheese; add cream and remaining cheese to sauce. Stir until cheese is melted. Remove from heat; add remaining butter, small amount at a time, rotating skillet to effect gradual melting. Pour sauce over fillets and spinach; sprinkle with reserved cheese. Bake quickly at 425 degrees until lightly browned; may be placed under broiler until brown. Yield: 6 servings.

Janet Christensen
The Boston Herald Traveler

59

San Pedro Fish Bake

SAN PEDRO FISH BAKE

> 1 3-lb. whole ocean perch or
>   red snapper
> 2 lge. onions, sliced
> 3 stalks celery, sliced
> 3 tomatoes, cut in wedges
> 1/4 c. minced parsley
> 1/2 c. fish or chicken broth
> 1/2 c. dry white wine
> 1 bay leaf
> 1/2 tsp. salt
> 1/4 tsp. pepper
> Paprika
> Lemon slices

Clean fish. Remove backbone, if desired; do not split fish. Spread onions, celery and tomatoes in shallow baking dish. Place fish over bed of vegetables; sprinkle with parsley. Add broth, wine and bay leaf; sprinkle with salt, pepper and paprika. Cover. Bake at 350 degrees for 30 to 45 minutes or until fish flakes with fork and vegetables are tender. Serve hot from baking dish or carefully lift onto platter,

arranging vegetables around fish. Garnish with lemon slices. Yield: 4-6 servings.

Jeanne Voltz
The Los Angeles Times

TROUT MEUNIERE

> 3 lb. trout fillets
> 1 c. milk
> Salt and pepper to taste
> 2 tbsp. flour
> 1/4 lb. butter, melted
> 1/2 c. chopped almonds
> 2 tsp. chopped parsley

Dip cleaned fillets into mixture of milk, salt and pepper; dip into flour to cover both sides. Place fillets in butter in saucepan. Fry until brown on both sides. Remove fillets to serving platter. Add almonds and parsley to butter; cook for 1 minute. Pour over fillets; serve immediately.

Rachel Daniel
The New Orleans Times-Picayune

FLOUNDER WITH CRAB STUFFING

> 6 3/4-lb. pan-dressed flounder
> Crab Stuffing
> 3/4 c. butter or margarine, melted
> 1/3 c. lemon juice
> 2 tsp. salt
> Paprika

Clean, wash and dry flounder; place on cutting board, light side down. Cut down center of fish along backbone from tail to about 1 inch from head end with sharp knife. Turn knife flat; cut flesh along both sides of backbone to tail, allowing knife to run over rib bones. Stuff with Crab Stuffing loosely. Combine butter, lemon juice and salt. Cut six 18-inch square pieces of heavy-duty aluminum foil; grease lightly. Place 2 teaspoons butter sauce on foil; place fish in sauce. Top each fish with 1 tablespoon sauce; sprinkle with paprika. Bring foil up over fish;

close all edges with tight double folds. Place on grill about 6 inches from moderately hot coals; cook for 25 to 30 minutes or until fish flakes easily when tested with fork. Yield: 6 servings.

CRAB STUFFING

1 lb. crab meat or 3 6 1/2 or 7-oz.
  cans crab meat
1/2 c. chopped onion
1/3 c. chopped celery
1/3 c. chopped green pepper
2 cloves of garlic, finely chopped
1/3 c. melted fat or oil
2 c. soft bread cubes
3 eggs, beaten
1 tbsp. chopped parsley
2 tsp. salt
1/2 tsp. pepper

Thaw crab meat, if frozen; drain. Remove any remaining shell or cartilage. Cook onion, celery, green pepper and garlic in fat until tender. Combine bread cubes, eggs, parsley, salt, pepper, cooked vegetables and crab meat; mix thoroughly.

Ann M. Criswell
The Houston Chronicle

PEPPERED EGGS AND SALMON

1 1-lb. can salmon, drained
3 strips bacon
2 tbsp. butter
1/2 c. chopped green onions
  with tops
1 green pepper, diced
1/2 tsp. salt
1/4 tsp. cayenne
6 eggs, lightly beaten
1/4 c. light cream
1 tsp. Worcestershire sauce

Flake salmon; set aside. Saute bacon in skillet until crisp; drain on absorbent paper. Crumble bacon. Pour bacon fat from skillet; melt butter in same skillet. Saute onions and green pepper for about 5 minutes or until onions are transparent. Add seasonings and salmon. Combine eggs, cream and Worcestershire sauce. Add to skillet; cook over moderate heat, stirring constantly, until eggs are just set but still creamy. Turn into serving dish; sprinkle with bacon. Yield: 4 servings.

Carol Voshall
The Phoenix Gazette

DIFFERENT BAKED SALMON

1 1-lb. can salmon or 1 lb.
  smoked salmon
3/4 c. sour cream
1 tbsp. minced onion
1 c. drained pineapple chunks
1/2 c. green pepper, cut in strips
1/8 tsp. pepper

Drain salmon. Remove skin and bones; separate into chunks. Combine remaining ingredients. Toss salmon with sour cream mixture just enough to mix slightly. Place in 1-quart casserole; cover. Bake at 350 degrees for 30 minutes. To use smoked salmon, freshen slightly by simmering in water to cover for about 5 minutes. Drain; cut in chunks. Yield: 4 servings.

Yvonne Rothert
The Oregonian

CUCUMBER SAUCE FOR SALMON

1/4 c. mayonnaise
1/4 c. heavy cream
1/4 c. chopped cucumber
2 tbsp. chopped onion
1 tsp. vinegar or lemon juice

Mix all ingredients together; serve over cold canned salmon for a delightful summer dish. Yield: 4 servings.

Mary Hart
The Minneapolis Tribune

FRIED RAZOR CLAMS

Clams, cleaned and drained
Dry bread or cracker crumbs
1 egg, beaten
1 tbsp. milk or water

Pick over clams to remove bits of shell. Roll in crumbs. Combine egg with milk; dip clams in egg mixture. Roll in crumbs again. Heat 1/4 to 1/2 inch fat in frying pan; add clams. Fat should be hot enough to brown one side of clam lightly in 2 or 3 minutes. Do not crowd pan. Turn and brown other side. Serve immediately. Long cooking makes clams tough. Serve with lemon wedges or with desired fish sauce.

Marjorie Anderson "Mary Cullen"
The Oregon Journal

STEAMED MUSSELS

5 lb. mussels about 4 in. long
2 c. water
8 sprigs of parsley, coarsely chopped
3 cloves of garlic, chopped
3 tbsp. olive oil
1/2 tsp. salt
Dash of pepper
2 tbsp. butter
Lemon Butter

Cover mussels with water; stir, using hand, so shells rub together thoroughly. Drain off water when cloudy. Repeat several times for about 1 hour and 30 minutes or until last soaking water is clear. This is the secret to well-flavored mussels. Pull off feathery beard on each mussel. Combine 2 cups water, parsley, garlic, olive oil, salt and pepper in large kettle; add mussels. Cover kettle; bring to a boil. Steam for 15 to 20 minutes or just till mussel shells open. Do not add more water. Do not overcook or meat will shrink and become tough and dry. Lift mussels into serving bowl. Add butter to broth in kettle. Spoon broth into bowls or mugs; serve separately. Serve mussels with Lemon Butter. Yield: 6 servings.

LEMON BUTTER

1 stick butter
1/4 c. lemon juice
1 tsp. salt

Melt butter in saucepan. Add lemon juice and salt; mix well. Yield: 3/4 cup butter.

Janet Beighle
The Cleveland Plain Dealer

CRAYFISH ETOUFFEE

6 tbsp. butter
2 c. onions, chopped
2 cloves of garlic, minced
1/2 c. green pepper, chopped
1 tsp. tomato puree
1/2 c. green onions, chopped
1/2 c. parsley, minced
2 c. celery, chopped
3 c. crayfish meat
2 tsp. Worcestershire sauce
Salt and pepper to taste
Hot pepper sauce to taste

Melt butter in iron skillet. Saute onions, garlic and green pepper; let simmer for about 10 to 15 minutes or until tender, stirring constantly. Add tomato puree; cook for another 5 minutes. Add green onions, parsley, celery and crayfish; add seasonings. Cook for about 15 to 20 minutes, stirring to keep from sticking. Remove from heat; let stand for about 30 minutes for seasonings to blend. Serve with rice. Yield: 6-8 servings.

Bettye Anding
The New Orleans States-Item

BEN LIN'S STEAMED CRABS

4 jumbo-sized crabs
2 slices fresh ginger
3 tbsp. soy sauce
1 tbsp. cider vinegar
2 tsp. sugar

Steam crabs for about 10 minutes or until shells turn red. Mince ginger; place in skillet. Add soy sauce, vinegar and sugar. Cook over low heat for several minutes, stirring constantly. Place mixture in dipping dish; serve crabs hot. Ginger is available in Chinese grocery stores.

Winifred Phillips
The Baltimore Sunpapers

CRAB CAKES

1 egg, beaten
1 tbsp. prepared mustard
1 tbsp. chopped parsley
1 tsp. Worcestershire sauce
Salt and pepper to taste
2 slices bread
1 lb. lump crab meat

Combine egg, mustard and seasonings. Trim bread; cut into small pieces. Soak well in egg mixture. Add crab meat; try not to break up. Form into cakes. Cook until brown in hot bacon fat. Yield: 6 large cakes.

Martha H. Schoeps
The Baltimore Sunpapers

SEAFOOD SOUFFLE

1   12-oz. pkg. frozen crab or
*   lobster Newburg*
1/2 c. shredded Swiss cheese
1 tbsp. sherry (opt.)
1/2 tsp. salt
Dash of pepper
4 egg yolks
5 egg whites

Preheat oven to 350 degrees. Heat crab according to package directions until thawed. Transfer to mixing bowl; add cheese, sherry, salt and pepper. Stir until cheese is melted. Beat egg yolks until light; slowly stir into slightly cooled crab mixture. Beat egg whites until stiff but not dry. Add 1 large spoonful beaten whites to crab mixture; stir until well mixed. Gently fold in remaining whites with rubber spatula. Pour into buttered 1 1/2-quart souffle dish. Set in shallow pan containing 1 inch hot water. Bake for 35 to 40 minutes or until center of souffle no longer wobbles when dish is shaken gently. Yield: 4 servings.

Carol Voshall
The Phoenix Gazette

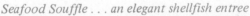

Seafood Souffle . . . an elegant shellfish entree

Lobster Cantonese . . . rich seafood on bed of rice

LOBSTER CANTONESE

>2 lb. fresh or frozen lobster-tails
>1/4 lb. ground pork
>1 clove of garlic, sliced
>1/4 c. melted butter or oil
>1/2 c. sliced green onions
>2 beef bouillon cubes
>2 c. boiling water
>2 tbsp. cornstarch
>1 tbsp. soy sauce
>1 tsp. ground ginger
>1/2 tsp. salt
>1/4 tsp. sugar
>1 egg, slightly beaten

Cut lobster-tails in half lengthwise, then crosswise into 1 1/2-inch pieces. Fry pork and garlic in butter until brown. Add onions and lobster. Cook for 10 to 15 minutes longer or until lobster is tender, stirring occasionally. Combine remaining ingredients except egg; add to lobster mixture. Cook until thick and clear, stirring constantly. Stir in egg. Yield: 6 servings.

Elaine Tait
The Philadelphia Inquirer

CLEO'S FRA DIAVOLO

>6 1-lb. lobsters, split
>3/4 c. olive oil
>3 c. tomato sauce
>6 tbsp. finely chopped parsley
>3 tbsp. minced garlic
>3/4 tsp. oregano
>1 tsp. salt
>Freshly ground pepper

Saute lobsters, cut side down, in oil for 5 minutes. Arrange lobsters, cut side up, in large roasting pans. Combine remaining ingredients; spoon over lobsters. Add 1/4 inch water; cover pans tightly. Cook over low heat for 30 minutes. Yield: 6 servings.

Joan Babbage
The Newark Evening News

OYSTER PATTIES

>4 doz. oysters and liquid
>2 tbsp. butter
>1 med. onion, grated
>1 tbsp. flour
>1/2 c. chopped mushrooms and
> liquid

Salt and pepper
Dash of cayenne pepper
2 tbsp. chopped parsley
1/4 tsp. lemon juice
12 patty shells

Place oysters and liquid in saucepan. Bring to a boil; simmer for 10 minutes. Melt butter in saucepan. Add onion; blend in flour until smooth. Add mushrooms, salt, pepper, cayenne pepper, parsley, lemon juice and oysters; cook for 5 minutes. Pour into patty shells. Bake in 425-degree oven for 15 minutes. Yield: 12 servings.

Rachel Daniel
The New Orleans Times-Picayune

OYSTER FRITTERS

1/2 c. flour, sifted
2 tsp. baking powder
Salt and pepper
2 eggs, beaten
1 pt. select oysters
Cooking fat

Combine dry ingredients; sift into beaten eggs. Beat into a smooth batter. Drop oysters, one at a time, into batter. Fry in hot fat in small saucepan or skillet. Yield: 4 servings.

Martha H. Schoeps
The Baltimore Sun

MRS. RALPH CIOFFI'S SCALLOPED OYSTERS

1 1/2 c. coarsely crushed saltines
1/2 c. melted margarine
1/4 tsp. pepper
Dash of cayenne pepper
1 tsp. paprika
1 tsp. parsley flakes
2 8-oz. can oysters
1 c. light cream

Combine crackers, margarine and seasonings; arrange 1/2 of the crumb mixture in shallow 1-quart baking dish. Drain oysters; reserve liquid. Arrange oysters on crumbs; sprinkle with remaining crumbs. Combine oyster

liquid with cream. Pour over crumbs. Bake in moderate 375-degree oven for 35 to 40 minutes.

Joan Babbage
The Newark Evening News

PAELLA

1 3-lb. (about) broiler-fryer
1 1/4 tsp. salt
1/2 tsp. paprika
4 tbsp. cooking oil or butter
1/2 lb. ham, diced
1 med. onion, chopped
1/2 c. diced pepper
1 16-oz. can peas
1 12-oz. bottle beer
1/2 tsp. hot pepper sauce
2 bouillon cubes
1/4 tsp. saffron
1 1/2 c. rice
6 mussels
6 clams
1/2 lb. cooked and cleaned shrimp
2 pimentos, cut in pieces

Cut chicken into serving pieces. Sprinkle chicken with 1 teaspoon salt and paprika. Heat oil in skillet; brown chicken. Remove to baking dish with tight-fitting cover. Cook ham in skillet; add to chicken. Cook onion and pepper in skillet until onion is tender but not brown. Drain liquid from peas; add liquid to beer. Add enough water to make 3 cups; add pepper sauce. Stir into skillet, scraping brown particles from bottom of pan. Add bouillon cubes, saffron and remaining 1/4 teaspoon salt. Heat to boiling; pour over chicken and ham. Sprinkle rice over chicken; stir to moisten rice. Cover. Bake at 350 degrees for 25 minutes. Uncover; toss lightly. Arrange mussels, clams, shrimp, pimentos and peas on top of rice mixture. Cover; return to oven for 10 minutes longer. Yield: 6 servings.

Jane Benet
The San Francisco Chronicle

SCALLOPS A LA JIMMY

2 lb. scallops
Butter
1 tbsp. bread crumbs
Pinch of garlic salt
Pinch of dry mustard
Pinch of paprika
Few drops of sherry
Freshly squeezed lemon

Preheat broiler for 20 minutes. Slice large scallops horizontally through center. Place scallops in ovenproof platter containing small amount of butter. Combine bread crumbs, garlic salt, mustard and paprika; spread over scallops. Dot with butter. Place under broiler for 5 to 7 minutes or until brown. Turn oven off; let scallops heat through for about 3 minutes longer. Add sherry. Serve hot with lemon. May serve as entree or hors d'oeuvres. This recipe is by Jimmy Doulos of Jimmy's Harborside Restaurant in Boston. Yield: 4 servings.

Janet Christensen
The Boston Herald Traveler

SHRIMP FIESTA

2 lb. fresh shrimp
1   12-oz. bottle or can beer or ale
1/2 onion
1 sprig of parsley
1 lemon wedge
1 bay leaf
1 tsp. salt
2 tbsp. butter
2 tbsp. flour
1   8-oz. can tomato sauce
4 tbsp. chopped scallions
1/4 tsp. hot pepper sauce
1/4 tsp. nutmeg
Pinch of sugar

Peel and devein shrimp. Combine beer, onion, parsley, lemon, bay leaf and salt in kettle; bring to a boil. Add shrimp; bring to a boil again. Reduce heat; simmer for 5 minutes. Strain liquid; reserve. Melt butter in skillet; add flour and stir to smooth paste. Add reserved shrimp liquid, tomato sauce, scallions, pepper sauce, nutmeg and sugar. Cook, stirring constantly, until thickens and comes to a boil. Add shrimp; reheat. Serve with hot buttered noodles. Yield: 4-6 servings.

Ann M. Criswell
The Houston Chronicle

SHRIMPETTI

2 tbsp. butter
1/3 c. olive oil
1 med. onion, chopped
1 clove of garlic, pureed
1   10 1/2-oz. can tomato soup
1/2 c. water
1 tbsp. chopped parsley
1 tsp. salt
1 lb. med. shrimp, shelled and
   deveined
1   8-oz. pkg. spaghetti
Grated Parmesan cheese
Parsley

Heat butter and oil in heavy saucepan. Add onion and garlic; cook for 3 minutes or until onion is yellow. Stir in tomato soup, water, parsley and salt. Simmer for 10 minutes or until slightly thick. Add shrimp, cut into bite-sized pieces. Cook for 5 minutes. Cook spaghetti according to package directions; place on serving platter. Serve shrimp on spaghetti; sprinkle with Parmesan cheese. Garnish with parsley. Yield: 4 servings.

Alice Petersen
The New York News

SCAMPI

2 lb. jumbo shrimp
2 (or more) cloves of garlic
2 tsp. salt
1 tsp. dry mustard
1/4 tsp. pepper
4 tbsp. finely chopped parsley
1/3 c. lemon juice
1/2 c. olive oil

Shrimp Creole . . . New Orleans style

Shell and devein shrimp, leaving tails intact. Split shrimp almost through for 2/3 of the length from inner arc, leaving halves connected at tail, using sharp knife. Flatten split portion. Tail will curl in broiling. Combine pureed or finely chopped garlic with salt, mustard and pepper; add parsley, lemon juice and olive oil. Arrange shrimp in single layer in large shallow dish; spoon oil mixture over shrimp carefully. Cover with plastic wrap or aluminum foil; place in refrigerator to marinate for 2 hours. Arrange shrimp in shallow broiling pan; spoon on marinade. Place in preheated broiler about 4 inches from source of heat. Broil for 6 to 8 minutes or until shrimp turn pink and are lightly browned. Do not overcook. Serve immediately. Yield: 4 servings.

Ella Elvin
The New York News

SHRIMP CREOLE NEW ORLEANS

3 qt. boiling water
3 tbsp. lemon juice
2 tbsp. salt
4 sprigs of parsley
1 bay leaf
1 clove of garlic, peeled
1 stalk celery, cut
2 lb. fresh shrimp, peeled and deveined
2 tbsp. olive oil
2 lge. shallots, minced
1/2 green pepper, chopped
Salt, pepper and cayenne
2 med. tomatoes, peeled
2 8-oz. cans tomato sauce
1/4 c. sherry
1/4 c. butter
2 tbsp. chopped parsley
4 c. hot rice

Combine water, lemon juice, salt, parsley sprigs, bay leaf, garlic and celery. Bring to a boil. Add shrimp. Cover; simmer for 5 minutes or until shrimp are pink and tender. Drain. Heat olive oil in saucepan about 20 minutes before serving; add shallots and green pepper. Heat until tender but not brown. Add salt, pepper and cayenne to taste. Stir and cook for 1 to 2 minutes. Add finely chopped tomatoes and tomato sauce. Simmer for about 10 minutes. Add shrimp; simmer for 5 minutes. Add sherry, butter and chopped parsley just before serving. Serve over mound of fluffy rice. Yield: 6 servings.

Patricia Williams
The Cincinnati Enquirer

Delicious Sidedishes of Fresh Garden Beauty
That Add Sparkle to Your Meals

*C*onsider the lowly vegetable. Long scorned by
steak-and-baked-potato men as something to
be endured for nutrition's sake, vegetables have
now come alive.

*Vegetables now appear with intriguing sauces, with
spices, with nuts, with mushrooms, with pearl onions.
No longer are vegetables overcooked. No longer do
vegetables just lie there. Now they have zing.*

*You can make your mark as a great chef by fixing veg-
etables that compete with the steak or the roast
for attention and applause. The secrets of making
vegetable dishes that are outstanding are explained
in flawless recipes by America's leading newspaper
food editors on the following pages.*

*These editors give you recipes for Louisiana's Creole
Red Beans, lovely Empress Asparagus, colorful Copper
Pennies, steaming Broccoli with Walnut Butter, old
fashioned Corn Pudding, a beautiful Broccoli Puff,
Stuffed Eggplant Parmigiana, Onion Pie and many others.*

Vegetables

69

ARTICHOKE BOTTOMS AND SPINACH AU GRATIN

2 sm. cans or jars artichoke
  bottoms
1 tbsp. sweet butter
3 pkg. frozen chopped spinach
Salt
Freshly ground pepper
3/4 c. heavy cream
1 c. grated Swiss cheese

Preheat oven to 350 degrees. Drain and halve artichoke bottoms; saute slowly in butter. Cook spinach according to package directions; drain well. Season to taste. Mix spinach and cream together. Place artichoke hearts in bottom of shallow baking dish; top with creamed spinach. Sprinkle cheese over top. Bake for 45 minutes.

Patricia Williams
The Cincinnati Enquirer

EMPRESS ASPARAGUS

2 9-oz. pkg. frozen asparagus
  spears
1 can bean sprouts, drained
2 cans onion rings
2 10 1/2-oz. cans cream of
  mushroom soup
2 tsp. soy sauce
1 c. slivered almonds

Preheat oven to 350 degrees. Cook asparagus according to package directions; drain. Alternate layers of asparagus, bean sprouts and onion rings in buttered casserole, ending with onion rings. Mix soup and soy sauce together; pour over vegetables. Sprinkle lightly with almond slivers. Bake for 25 minutes. Yield: 6 servings.

Janice Okun
The Buffalo Evening News

MISSION GARDEN BLUE LAKES

1 1-lb. can cut Blue Lake
  green beans

1/4 c. butter or margarine
1 tbsp. chopped green onion
1 tsp. lemon juice
1/4 tsp. seasoned salt
1 tsp. soy sauce
1/4 c. sliced radishes
2 tbsp. toasted slivered almonds

Drain beans. Melt butter in skillet. Add onion; cook until tender-crisp. Stir in lemon juice, seasoned salt, soy sauce and radishes; heat, stirring, for several minutes. Add beans; heat through. Stir in almonds. Spoon into serving dish. Yield: 4 servings.

Julie Benell
The Dallas Morning News

CREOLE RED BEANS

2 c. dried red kidney beans
1/2 lb. diced ham
1 tbsp. shortening
1 green pepper, minced
1 clove of garlic, minced
2 onions, chopped
Minced celery leaves
1 tbsp. flour

Soak red beans overnight. Brown ham in shortening; add green pepper, garlic, onions and celery leaves. Sprinkle with flour; saute until onions are transparent. Add beans and enough hot water to cover; cook over low heat for about 2 hours, stirring occasionally to prevent sticking. Serve over hot rice with Dijon mustard, if desired. Yield: 8 servings.

Bettye Anding
The New Orleans State-Item

RED BEANS AND RICE

2 c. red beans
6 c. water
Salt and pepper
2 c. diced ham, salt pork or
  smoked sausage
1/4 c. bacon drippings
1 c. onions, chopped

2 cloves of garlic, minced
1/4 c. parsley

Soak beans in water for about 30 minutes; cook slowly for several hours until tender. Add salt and pepper to taste. Fry ham in bacon drippings. Add onions and garlic; cook until transparent. Add to cooked beans; stir in parsley. Remove about 1 cup beans; mash or put through sieve. Return to bean pot to thicken juice. Pour in additional boiling water, if needed. Serve over rice.

Rachel Daniel
The New Orleans Times-Picayune

SPICY BAKED BEANS

1 lb. navy beans
1 qt. water
1 1-lb. 3-oz. can tomatoes
2 tbsp. butter or margarine
1 clove of garlic
1 onion, chopped
1/2 c. chopped green pepper
1 c. chopped celery
1/4 tsp. ginger
1/3 c. molasses
1 tsp. salt
1/4 tsp. pepper
5 slices bacon

Combine beans and water; soak overnight. Add tomatoes to bean mixture; cook for about 1 hour and 30 minutes or until beans are tender. Melt butter in skillet. Add garlic, onion, green pepper and celery; cook until vegetables are tender and lightly browned. Remove and discard garlic; stir vegetables into beans. Mix ginger, molasses, salt and pepper into beans. Turn bean mixture into 2-quart casserole; top with bacon slices. Cover casserole. Bake in 300-degree oven for 2 hours. Remove cover; bake until bacon is crisp or for about 15 minutes. Yield: 6 servings.

Cyrilla Riley
The Detroit News

QUICK ORANGE SAUCE FOR BEETS

1/4 c. sugar
2 tbsp. flour
1/2 tsp. salt
1/2 c. orange juice
1 tbsp. grated orange rind

Blend sugar, flour and salt together; gradually add orange juice, stirring until smooth. Add orange rind. Cook over moderate heat, stirring, until thickened. Serve over cooked beets. Yield: About 1 cup sauce.

Helen Dollaghan
The Denver Post

Spicy Baked Beans
. . . a perfect barbecue accompaniment

SPICY BEETS

1/4 c. vinegar
1 onion, finely chopped
1 tsp. salt
1 tsp. sugar
1/4 tsp. dry mustard
1 tsp. Worcestershire sauce
1   1-lb. can sliced beets

Combine vinegar, onion, salt, sugar, mustard and Worcestershire sauce in saucepan. Bring to a boil; pour over beets. Serve hot or cold. Yield: 4 servings.

Cyrilla Riley
The Detroit News

BROCCOLI PUFF

4 pkg. frozen chopped broccoli
6 tbsp. butter or margarine
6 tbsp. flour
3 c. milk
Salt and pepper to taste
1 tsp. Worcestershire sauce
1/8 tsp. dry mustard
3 eggs, separated
Parmesan cheese

Cook broccoli according to package directions; drain. Melt butter; stir in flour. Add milk slowly; cook, stirring constantly, until thickened. Add salt, pepper, Worcestershire sauce and mustard. Add small amount of sauce to beaten egg yolks, beating constantly; stir egg yolk mixture into sauce. Fold in stiffly beaten egg whites; fold in broccoli. Pour into buttered 2-quart casserole; top with Parmesan cheese generously. Bake in 325-degree oven for 30 minutes. Yield: 8 servings.

Jean Thwaite
The Atlanta Constitution

BROCCOLI WITH WALNUT BUTTER

1 1/2 lb. broccoli
3 tbsp. butter or margarine
1/4 tsp. ground ginger
Dash of nutmeg
2 tbsp. chopped walnuts

Wash broccoli. Slit thick stems up to flowerets or cut stems in thin diagonal slices. Cook, covered, for 8 to 10 minutes in 1/3 cup boiling, salted water. Melt butter; add ginger, nutmeg and walnuts. Drain broccoli; toss with butter mixture. Yield: 4 servings.

Jeanne Voltz
The Los Angeles Times

COPPER PENNIES

2 lb. peeled carrots, sliced thin
1 sm. green pepper, sliced
1 med. onion, sliced thin
1 can tomato soup
1/2 c. salad oil
3/4 c. sugar
3/4 c. vinegar
1 tsp. prepared mustard
1 tsp. Worcestershire sauce

Cook carrot slices in boiling salted water until tender; let cool. Layer carrots, green pepper rings and onion rings alternately in shallow bowl. Combine remaining ingredients; pour over onion rings. Let stand in refrigerator for several hours or overnight. Yield: 4-6 servings.

Julie Benell
The Dallas Morning News

GREEN CAULIFLOWER

1 head cauliflower
2 avocados
Salt and pepper to taste
Dash of vinegar (opt.)
Sour cream or mayonnaise (opt.)

Cook and drain cauliflower. Place on serving plate. Puree avocados; season with salt, pepper and vinegar. Blend with sour cream. Frost cauliflower completely with avocado mixture. Cut cauliflower into wedges to serve.

Dorothee Polson
The Arizona Republic

PANCHO SAUCE FOR CAULIFLOWER

1 tbsp. butter or margarine
1 tbsp. flour
1 1/2 c. milk
1/2 c. smooth peanut butter
1/4 lb. process American cheese,
  cubed
Cooked cauliflower

Melt butter; blend in flour. Cook several minutes over moderate heat, stirring. Stir in milk gradually; bring to a boil, stirring constantly. Boil for 1 minute. Blend in peanut butter and cheese, stirring until melted and well blended. Serve over cauliflower. Yield: 2 cups.

Helen Dollaghan
The Denver Post

CORN PUDDING

2 c. cooked or canned whole
  kernel corn, drained
3 eggs, slightly beaten
2 c. milk, scalded
1 tbsp. melted butter
1 tsp. sugar
1 tsp. salt

Combine all ingredients; turn into greased 1 1/2-quart casserole. Set in shallow pan filled with hot water. Bake in 350-degree oven for about 45 minutes or until knife inserted in center comes out clean. Let stand for 10 minutes at room temperature; center will firm up. Yield: About 6 servings.

Helen Civelli Brown
The San Francisco Examiner

MOTHER'S SCALLOPED CORN

1 1-lb. can cream-style corn
1/2 c. milk
1 egg, well beaten
6 soda crackers, crushed
2 tbsp. minced green pepper
2 tbsp. minced onion
1 tsp. Worcestershire sauce
1/2 tsp. salt
1 tbsp. butter

Mix all ingredients except butter. Pour into greased 8-inch pie plate or baking dish; dot with butter. Bake at 350 degrees for 20 to 25 minutes. Yield: 4-6 servings.

Yvonne Rothert
The Oregonian

Corn Pudding . . . a delicious all-American favorite

STUFFED EGGPLANT PARMIGIANA

2 sm. eggplant
1 lb. Italian sausage
1   1-lb. can tomatoes
1 can tomato paste
2 tbsp. minced parsley
1 tbsp. minced onion
1 clove of garlic, minced
1/2 tsp. salt
1/2 tsp. crushed oregano
1 c. shredded mozzarella cheese
1/2 c. shredded Parmesan cheese

Preheat oven to 350 degrees. Cut eggplant in half. Scoop out pulp; dice. Remove casing from sausage. Brown sausage in skillet; drain on paper towels. Drain excess fat from skillet; combine sausage, tomatoes, tomato paste, parsley, onion, garlic and seasonings in skillet. Cover; simmer for 15 minutes. Add eggplant pulp; cover. Simmer for 15 minutes longer. Place eggplant shells in 13 x 9 1/2 x 2-inch baking dish; fill shells half full with sausage mixture. Sprinkle with mozzarella cheese. Heap remaining sausage mixture in shells; sprinkle with Parmesan cheese. Bake, uncovered, for 30 minutes. Garnish with hot peppers, if desired. Yield: 4 servings.

Martha H. Schoeps
The Baltimore Sunpapers

EGGPLANT CREOLE

1 med. eggplant
3 tbsp. butter
3 tbsp. flour
3 lge. tomatoes, peeled and
*   chopped*
1 sm. green pepper, chopped
1 sm. onion, chopped
1 tsp. salt
1 tbsp. brown sugar
1/2 bay leaf
2 cloves
Bread crumbs or Parmesan cheese

Peel eggplant; cut into bite-sized cubes. Cook for 10 minutes in boiling, salted water; drain. Place in buttered casserole. Melt butter in skillet. Add flour; mix well. Add remaining ingredients except bread crumbs; cook for 5 minutes. Remove bay leaf and cloves. Pour over eggplant; cover with bread crumbs. Bake at 350 degrees for 30 minutes. This has a Greek hint to it and is very rich. It can be served with lamb, but is a favorite with chicken basted with lemon, sherry and butter on the barbecue grill. Yield: 6 servings.

Kay Jarvis
The San Diego Evening Tribune

STUFFED MIRLITONS

4 mirlitons or eggplant
1 c. soft bread crumbs
1 lge. onion, finely chopped
1 clove of garlic, minced
3 tbsp. butter
1/2 tsp. salt
Pepper to taste
1 egg, well beaten
1 tsp. chopped parsley
1 sprig of thyme

1/2 lb. cooked shrimp, coarsely
    chopped
1/2 c. buttered bread crumbs

Simmer mirlitons in salted water until tender. Cut each in half; remove seeds. Spoon out pulp carefully; reserve shells. Chop pulp; add soft bread crumbs. Saute onion and garlic in butter over medium heat until tender, about 5 minutes. Stir in pulp mixture, salt and pepper; cook for 5 minutes, stirring frequently. Cool. Add egg, parsley, thyme and shrimp; mix thoroughly. Fill reserved shells; cover with buttered crumbs. Bake in 375-degree oven for 25 minutes. Mirlitons are called chayotes in Florida. Yield: 8 servings.

Rachel Daniel
The New Orleans Times-Picayune

STUFFED MUSHROOMS

2 lb. mushrooms
Melted butter or margarine
1 sm. onion, minced
2 tbsp. butter or margarine
1/4 c. all-purpose flour
1/4 tsp. salt
1/2 c..milk
1/2 c. sour cream
1 egg
1 c. chopped cooked and drained
    spinach
1/2 c. grated American cheese
1/4 c. chopped cooked bacon
1/2 c. chopped ripe olives
Nutmeg
Parmesan cheese

Clean and stem mushrooms; brush inside and out with melted butter. Cook onion in 2 tablespoons butter until soft. Blend flour and salt into onion; add milk, stirring constantly, until thickened and smooth. Add sour cream, egg, spinach, American cheese, bacon and olives. Stuff mushrooms with mixture. Dust with nutmeg and Parmesan cheese. Bake at 350 degrees

for about 5 to 10 minutes or until heated through. Serve hot.

Margaret C. Bowers
The Oakland Tribune

OKRA AND TOMATOES

1/4 lb. ham, diced
2 tbsp. bacon drippings
1 c. chopped onion
1 lb. okra, sliced 1/8 in. thick
1 1/2 c. chopped tomatoes
Dash of sugar
1 tsp. salt
1/4 tsp. pepper

Saute ham in large frypan over medium heat for 5 minutes. Remove ham; heat bacon drippings. Add onion, okra and ham. Fry for about 45 minutes until okra ceases to rope, adding water, one tablespoon at a time, as needed. Do not stir; turn with large pancake spatula at 10 minute intervals. Add tomatoes, sugar and seasonings to taste. Cover; simmer for 15 minutes. Yield: 4 servings.

Bettye Anding
The New Orleans States-Item

ONION PIE

1 unbaked 9-in. pastry shell
4 med. onions, sliced
4 slightly beaten eggs
2 c. sour cream
1 tsp. salt
1/2 tsp. red hot sauce
1/2 tsp. tarragon

Chill pastry shell. Preheat oven to 450 degrees. Saute onions until golden and transparent; drain. Arrange onions in pastry shell. Stir eggs into sour cream; season with salt, red hot sauce and tarragon. Pour over onions. Bake for 10 minutes. Reduce oven temperature to 350 degrees; bake for 40 to 45 minutes longer or until filling is set. Yield: 6-8 servings.

Cyrilla Riley
The Detroit News

HELEN CORBITT'S PICKLED BLACK-EYED PEAS

2 No. 2 cans cooked dried
*   black-eyed peas*
1 c. salad oil
1/4 c. wine vinegar
1 clove of garlic
1/4 c. thinly sliced onion
1/2 tsp. salt
Cracked or freshly ground pepper

Drain liquid from peas; place peas in pan or bowl. Add remaining ingredients; mix thoroughly. Place in jar; cover. Refrigerate for 1 day; remove garlic. Refrigerate for 2 days to 2 weeks before serving. Red kidney beans and garbanzos may be used. These make a delightful addition to a cocktail buffet for a change of pace, but you do need a plate and fork. Yield: 6 servings.

Julie Benell
The Dallas Morning News

MEATBALL STUFFED POTATOES

4 lge. baking potatoes
3/4 lb. ground lean beef
3/4 c. soft bread crumbs
1 tbsp. instant minced onion
1 tsp. seasoned salt
2/3 c. sauterne or rose wine
1/3 c. catsup
1 tbsp. chutney sauce (opt.)
1/4 c. Chablis, sauterne or other
*   white wine*
1/4 c. light cream
1 tsp. seasoned salt
1/4 c. grated Parmesan cheese

Scrub potatoes; dry and oil lightly. Bake in 450-degree oven for about 45 to 50 minutes or until done. Combine beef, bread crumbs, onion, 1 teaspoon seasoned salt, 1/3 cup sauterne and 2 tablespoons catsup. Shape into tiny meatballs. Arrange in shallow pan. Bake in 450-degree oven for 15 min-

utes or until done. Combine remaining 1/3 cup sauterne, catsup and chutney sauce; stir into meatballs. Remove potatoes from oven; split lengthwise. Carefully remove potato pulp, leaving 1/4-inch shell. Press pulp through sieve; beat until smooth with 1/4 cup Chablis, cream, 1 teaspoon seasoned salt and cheese. Spoon a small amount of potato into bottom of each shell; fill with meatballs. Spoon or press remaining potato through pastry tube to fill shell and surround meatballs. Place under broiler until lightly browned. Yield: 4 servings.

Margaret C. Bowers
The Oakland Tribune

POTATO PANCAKES

1/4 c. milk
1 egg, beaten
3 tbsp. flour
1/4 tsp. baking powder
1 tbsp. grated onion
1 tsp. salt
2 c. finely grated potatoes

Mix first 6 ingredients; add potatoes, mixing well. Drop by tablespoonfuls, 2 inches apart, onto well-greased griddle. Cook until crisp and browned on both sides. Serve with applesauce. Yield: 8-10 pancakes.

Martha H. Schoeps
The Baltimore Sun

DIETER'S DELIGHT LEMON POTATOES

2 lb. Idaho potatoes
1 lge. onion, coarsely chopped
2 tbsp. flour
4 tbsp. butter or margarine
1/4 c. fresh chopped parsley
1/4 tsp. nutmeg
Salt and pepper
Grated rind and juice of 1 lemon

Peel potatoes; cut into large pieces. Parboil in boiling salted water for 4 minutes. Toss with remaining ingredients except lemon juice. Transfer to 2-quart casserole. Bake in 450-degree oven until potatoes are tender. Squeeze lemon juice over top just before serving. Yield: 6 servings.

Ann M. Criswell
The Houston Chronicle

DELMONICO POTATOES

8 or 9 red potatoes
1 c. milk
1/2 c. whipping cream
1/2 lb. sharp Cheddar cheese
1 tsp. salt
1 tsp. dry mustard
Dash of pepper
Dash of nutmeg

Cook potatoes in boiling, salted water until tender. Cool; peel and slice. Place in buttered casserole. Combine remaining ingredients in saucepan. Heat and stir until cheese is melted and sauce is smooth. Pour over potatoes. Cover; refrigerate overnight. Bake in preheated 325-degree oven for 1 hour. Yield: 10-12 servings.

Patricia Williams
The Cincinnati Enquirer

SWISS CHEESE-NUTMEG POTATOES

1 3/4 c. water
1/4 c. butter
1 tsp. salt
1 c. cold milk
1   4 1/8-oz. pkg. instant whipped
*   potato flakes*
6 oz. Swiss cheese, shredded

Bring water, butter and salt to a boil in medium saucepan. Remove from heat; add milk and nutmeg. Add potato flakes; stir gently until soft and moist. Add half the cheese; beat briskly with fork or wire whip until cheese is melted. Turn into ovenproof dish.

Sprinkle with remaining cheese. Broil until lightly flecked with brown. Yield: 4 servings.

Yvonne Rothert
The Oregonian

Delmonico Potatoes

MRS. JANE SCHUYLER'S TIPSY SWEET POTATOES

6 med. sweet potatoes
1 c. hot milk
Sugar to taste
1/2 stick butter
1/2 c. walnuts
Salt to taste
1 c. bourbon
Marshmallows

Peel and boil potatoes until done; drain. Mash well. Mix in milk, sugar, butter, walnuts, salt and bourbon. Place in greased baking dish; top with marshmallows. Bake at 350 degrees for about 30 minutes or until marshmallows are golden brown. Yield: 6-8 servings.

Joan Babbage
The Newark Evening News

SWEET POTATO-BANANA CASSEROLE

1   1-lb. can sweet potatoes, sliced
2 lge. bananas, sliced
1/4 c. brown sugar
1/4 c. butter
Toasted shredded coconut

Preheat oven to 350 degrees. Arrange alternate rows of sweet potato and banana slices in single layer in buttered shallow baking dish. Sprinkle with sugar; dot with butter. Bake for 30 minutes. Garnish with coconut. Yield: 4 servings.

Patricia Williams
The Cincinnati Enquirer

FRIED RICE

3 c. cooled cooked rice
1/4 tsp. salt
1/4 c. diced roast pork
1/2 c. finely diced celery
1/3 c. diced green onions
1/2 c. drained canned bean sprouts
1 egg, beaten
2 tbsp. soy sauce
Dash of pepper

Heat rice and salt in well-greased skillet. Add pork, celery, green onions, bean sprouts and egg. Cook and stir for 3 minutes over high heat. Add small amount of shortening if rice tends to stick. Add soy sauce and pepper. Cook and stir for 1 minute longer. Yield: 4-6 servings.

Jeanne Voltz
The Los Angeles Times

RICE VERDE

3/4 to 1 lb. Monterey Jack cheese
1 pt. sour cream
1 can green chilies, chopped
3 c. cooked seasoned rice
1/4 c. Cheddar or Parmesan
    cheese, grated

Cut Jack cheese into strips. Combine sour cream and chilies. Arrange layers of rice, sour cream mixture and cheese strips in baking dish until all ingredients are used, ending with rice. Bake at 350 degrees for about 20 minutes or until heated through. Sprinkle top with grated cheese; bake about 10 minutes longer or until cheese is melted. Yield: 6-8 servings.

Dorothee Polson
The Arizona Republic

WILD RICE CASSEROLE

4 strips bacon
1/2 c. chopped onion
1/4 c. chopped green pepper
1/2 lb. fresh mushrooms, chopped
2 tbsp. melted butter
1 can cream of mushroom soup
1/2 c. dry white wine
1/2 c. coarsely chopped ripe olives
1 tsp. celery salt
3 c. cooked wild rice
2 c. cooked white rice

Fry bacon until crisp. Remove from skillet. Saute onion, green pepper and mushrooms in drippings for 5 minutes. Combine all ingredients; place in casserole. Add more liquid if mixture seems dry. Cover. Bake at 325 degrees for 1 hour. Yield: 6-8 servings.

Mary Hart
The Minneapolis Tribune

CHEESE-SPINACH CASSEROLE

1 pt. creamed cottage cheese
3 eggs
1/4 lb. American cheese
1/4 c. butter
1   10-oz. pkg. frozen spinach
3 tbsp. flour

Combine cottage cheese and eggs. Cut American cheese and butter into coarse pieces; add to cottage cheese mixture. Snip frozen spinach irregularly with kitchen shears into cheese mixture. Add flour; stir until thoroughly blended. Pour into well-greased

1 1/2-quart casserole. Bake at 350 degrees for about 1 hour or until set. Yield: 4-6 servings.

Helen Dollaghan
The Denver Post

ROSE KANG'S KOREAN-STYLE SPINACH

1 lb. spinach
2 tbsp. soy sauce
1 tsp. sesame or peanut oil
1 clove of garlic, chopped
1 scallion, chopped

Wash spinach; drain. Cook in boiling water until spinach turns light green; do not overcook. Rinse under cold water; squeeze water out gently. Cut into 2-inch lengths. Add soy sauce, sesame oil, garlic and scallion; mix well. well.

Joan Babbage
The Newark Evening News

PENNSYLVANIA DUTCH TOMATOES

1/2 lb. bacon
1/2 cube butter
1 sm. onion, minced fine
3 ripe firm tomatoes
1/3 c. brown sugar
2 tsp. cornstarch
1 8-oz. carton sour cream
1/3 tsp. salt
Chopped fresh parsley

Cut bacon into small squares; fry. Drain on paper toweling. Melt butter in separate skillet; saute onion until just softened. Slice tomatoes 3/4 inch thick; place edge to edge in onion mixture. Saute for 5 minutes, turning once. Place 1 teaspoon brown sugar on each tomato slice. Mix cornstarch with sour cream; place by spoonfuls around tomatoes. Simmer until slightly thickened. Season with salt. Sprinkle with parsley and crumbled bacon. Lift tomatoes and sour cream carefully onto shallow platter or serving dish. The sprinkling of fresh parsley and crisp bacon on tomatoes makes this a spectacularly eye-catching dish. It's rich so serve with a simple entree such as rib roast, pork loin or leg of lamb. Yield: 6 servings.

Kay Jarvis
The San Diego Evening Tribune

SUMMER SQUASH RING

6 to 8 med.-sized crookneck
*   squash or zucchini*
1/4 c. butter or margarine, melted
1 tsp. salt
Dash of pepper
1/8 tsp. cayenne (opt.)
1 tbsp. grated onion
3 eggs
1 tbsp. melted butter
1/4 c. packaged bread crumbs
2 10-oz. pkg. frozen peas, cooked
Sauteed whole mushrooms (opt.)

Wash squash. Cut about 8 thin slices; reserve for trim. Slice remaining squash; place in saucepan containing small amount of boiling salted water. Simmer for about 15 minutes or until tender; drain well. Put through sieve. Rinse sieve; return squash to sieve to drain thoroughly. Add 1/4 cup melted butter, seasonings and onion to eggs; beat well. Stir in 3 cups drained squash. Combine 1 tablespoon melted butter and bread crumbs; stir into squash mixture. Line bottom of oiled 1-quart ring mold with reserved squash slices; spoon squash mixture on top. Set mold in pan of hot water. Bake at 350 degrees for about 25 minutes or until firm. Place serving platter over mold; invert. Place bowl in center of mold; fill with peas. Circle with sauteed mushrooms, if desired, and trim with parsley. Yield: 6 servings.

Janet Beighle
The Cleveland Plain Dealer

Covered Dish Creations Made Quick
and Easy, Yet Taste Tempting, Too

*W*hen you want an unbeatable yet easy meal, con-
coct a tasty casserole. Most casseroles are
quick and simple to prepare, and they allow the cook
wide scope for her imagination. They also provide
delectable ways to use leftover meats and vegetables.

In a casserole you can combine all the necessary ingredients to serve your family a balanced meal in
one dish. A casserole is often a perfect answer when
unexpected guests arrive at mealtime.

On the pages that follow, you will find recipes for
many delicious main dish casseroles selected, compiled,
and carefully described by America's leading newspaper
food editors. Try such wonderful favorites as Italian
Lasagna, a special casserole of Beef and Wild Rice,
Chicken Masquerade, a Holiday Chicken dish, South
Pacific Chicken from the Islands, Turkey Marco Polo,
Spaghetti with Clam Sauce, Pears and Shrimp Oriental,
delicious Lobster Baked with Mushrooms, Cheese and
Bacon Strata, Quick Quiche and a lovely Cheese Souffle.

Main Dish Casseroles

DAUBE PROVENCALE
BEEF STEW IN WINE

> 3 lb. round of beef
> 1 tsp. salt
> 1/4 tsp. freshly ground pepper
> 1 whole allspice
> 1/4 c. wine vinegar
> 1 clove of garlic, crushed
> 4 c. red wine
> 2 tbsp. lard or butter
> 12 sm. white onions
> 1/2 lb. salt pork, diced
> 3 carrots, cut in 3/4-in. pieces
> 2 stalks celery, cut in 1/2-in. pieces
> 1 sm. bay leaf
> Pinch of thyme

Cut beef in 2-inch cubes; mix with salt, pepper, allspice, vinegar, garlic and 2 cups wine in large bowl. Let stand for 2 hours, turning beef once. Dry beef with paper towel. Strain marinade; reserve. Heat lard in heatproof casserole. Add onions, salt pork, carrots and celery; cook until slightly golden. Add beef; cook until beef is browned. Add bay leaf, thyme, reserved marinade and remaining wine; bring to a boil. Cover. Bake in 375-degree oven for 5 hours or until beef is very tender. Serve with Duchess potatoes spooned around the edge of heatproof serving platter, sprinkled with grated Swiss cheese and complete meal with tiny peas and mushrooms and/or a salad and French bread with more wine. The dry flavor of good red wine makes this stew very special. The marinating and long cooking time makes the beef stew meat just as good as more expensive meat. Canned or frozen small onions are just as good and more readily available than fresh white onions. Yield: 6 servings.

Eleanor Ostman
The St. Paul Dispatch-Pioneer Press

MRS. SMITH'S CHINESE HAMBURGER

> 1 c. chopped celery
> 1 c. chopped onion
> 2 tbsp. salad oil
> 1 1/2 lb. ground beef
> 1   1-lb. can bean sprouts
> 1 med. can mushrooms and liquid
> 1 sm. can water chestnuts, cut up
> 1/2 c. rice
> 2 cans cream of mushroom soup
> 2 tbsp. soy sauce
> 1 can Chinese noodles

Cook celery and onion in oil until tender. Add beef; cook until done. Drain bean sprouts; reserve 1/2 cup liquid. Place 1/2 of the beef mixture in casserole. Add 1/2 of the mushrooms and liquid; add 1/2 of the bean sprouts. Add 1/2 of the water chestnuts; add 1/2 of the rice. Repeat layers in same order. Mix soup, reserved bean sprout liquid and soy sauce; pour over top. Cover. Bake at 350 degrees for 30 minutes. Remove from oven; cover with noodles. Return to oven; bake for 30 minutes longer. Yield: 10-12 servings.

Dorothy Neighbors
The Seattle Times

Daube Provencale

Lasagna . . . a favorite dish from Italy

LASAGNA

1 lb. ground beef
3 cloves of garlic, minced
1 lb. Italian sausage, crumbled
1   8-oz. can tomato sauce
1   16-oz. can Italian-style
    tomatoes
3 tsp. salt
1/2 tsp. pepper
1 tsp. oregano
1 lb. lasagna noodles
4 qt. water
1 tbsp. cooking oil
1   6-oz. pkg. sliced mozzarella
    cheese
2   12-oz. cartons sm. curd
    cottage cheese
2 eggs
Grated Parmesan cheese

Preheat oven to 375 degrees. Cook beef, garlic and sausage in skillet until beef loses red color; drain off grease. Add tomato sauce, tomatoes, 1 teaspoon salt, pepper and oregano; simmer, covered, for about 1 hour. Cook noodles in boiling water to which remaining salt and cooking oil have been added; drain. Arrange half the noodles in greased large shallow baking dish; top with half the mozzarella cheese. Combine cottage cheese and eggs; mix well. Spoon half the cottage cheese mixture on mozzarella cheese; add half the meat mixture. Sprinkle with Parmesan cheese; repeat layers. Bake for 30 minutes. May be frozen before baking, if desired. Yield: 6-8 servings.

Helen Dollaghan
The Denver Post

BEEF AND WILD RICE CASSEROLE

3 tbsp. chopped onion
2 tbsp. butter
1 lb. ground beef
2/3 c. wild rice
1   10 1/2-oz. can cream of
    chicken soup
1/2 tsp. salt
1/2 tsp. onion salt
1/2 tsp. garlic salt
1/2 tsp. celery salt
1   4-oz. can mushrooms
Parmesan cheese

Saute onion in butter. Add ground beef; brown. Add remaining ingredients except cheese; place in 2-quart casserole. Sprinkle with Parmesan cheese. Bake at 350 degrees for 1 hour. Yield: 4-6 servings.

Jo Ann Vachule
The Fort Worth Star-Telegram

83

LIVER AND RICE CASSEROLE

1 lb. sliced liver
1/4 c. chopped green pepper
1/2 c. chopped celery
1 med. onion, diced
2 tbsp. drippings
1 8-oz. can tomato sauce
1 1-lb. can tomatoes
1 1/2 tsp. salt
1/2 tsp. pepper
1/8 tsp. thyme
3 c. cooked rice
1/2 c. shredded sharp Cheddar
  cheese

Cut liver into 1-inch squares. Cook with green pepper, celery and onion in drippings until liver is lightly browned and vegetables are tender. Pour off drippings. Add tomato sauce, tomatoes, salt, pepper, thyme and rice. Turn into greased 1 1/2-quart casserole; sprinkle cheese over top. Bake at 350 degrees for 20 to 30 minutes. Yield: 4-5 servings.

Jeanne Voltz
The Los Angeles Times

RAMSETTI

1 3/4 lb. veal
1/2 lb. pork
1 onion, chopped
1 sm. green pepper, chopped
2 10 3/4-oz. cans tomato soup
2 soup cans water
1 10-oz. pkg. noodles
1 4-oz. can mushrooms
1 c. grated Cheddar cheese

Chop veal and pork fine; brown in small amount of fat. Remove from skillet; saute vegetables in same skillet. Return meat to skillet; add soup and water. Cook, covered, over low heat until meat is done. Cook noodles according to package directions; add to meat mixture. Add mushrooms; mix well. Place in casserole; sprinkle

with cheese. Bake in 350-degree oven until cheese melts. Yield: 6 servings.

Jo Ann Vachule
The Fort Worth Star-Telegram

BEEF-PORK LOAF

1 lb. ground beef
1/2 lb. ground pork
1 egg
1 can steak sauce with mushrooms
1/2 c. crushed corn flakes
1/2 sm. onion, minced
1 tbsp. each salt and pepper
1/2 tsp. horseradish
3 tbsp. catsup

Combine all ingredients; mix well. Place into loaf pan. Bake in 350-degree oven for 1 hour. May be refrigerated overnight before baking, if desired; helps loaf hold shape and makes slicing easier. Yield: 6 servings.

Opal M. Crandall
The San Diego Union

PTA CASSEROLE

1/2 lb. pork
1/2 lb. veal
1 sm. pkg. noodles
1 or 2 green peppers, chopped
2 jars pimento, chopped
1 can peas, drained
1 can yellow corn, drained
1 can cream of mushroom or
  cream of chicken soup
1/2 lb. Cheddar or shorthorn
  cheese, grated
Ground pepper and salt to taste
1 10-cent pkg. potato chips,
  crushed

Have butcher grind pork and veal together. Prepare noodles according to package directions. Brown ground meats in large frying pan. Add noodles and remaining ingredients except potato chips; place in large casserole.

Sprinkle potato chips on top. Bake at 350 degrees for about 40 minutes. Best if refrigerated and reheated; recipe may be varied to desired taste. Yield: 6 generous servings.

Marjean Phillips Busby
The Kansas City Star and Times

CHICKEN MASQUERADE

1 can chicken with rice soup
2 soup cans water
1/2 tsp. salt
1 lb. boned lean pork tenderloin
8 oz. broken broad noodles
1 No. 303 can cream-style corn
2 pimentos, chopped
1 sm. green pepper, chopped
2 c. grated sharp natural cheese
Parmesan cheese

Combine soup, water and salt. Add pork; simmer, covered, until pork is tender, for 1 hour to 1 hour and 30 minutes. Cook noodles until partially done in boiling salted water, about 7 minutes. Remove pork from soup mixture; cut into 1-inch pieces. Set aside. Drain noodles; blanch. Bring soup mixture to a boil; add noodles. Reduce heat; cook until noodles are tender. Remove form heat; stir in pork, corn, pimentos, green pepper and sharp cheese. Blend well. Pour into greased 2-quart casserole; sprinkle with Parmesan cheese. Bake, covered, for 45 minutes at 375 degrees. Uncover; bake for 15 minutes longer.

Helen Dollaghan
The Denver Post

CHICKEN-RICE CASSEROLE

1 c. wild rice
1/2 c. chopped onions
1/2 c. butter or margarine
1/4 c. flour
1 4-oz. can sliced mushrooms
Chicken broth

1 1/2 c. light cream
3 c. cooked diced chicken
2 tbsp. parsley
1 1/2 tsp. salt
1/4 tsp. pepper
1/2 c. slivered almonds

Prepare wild rice according to package directions. Saute onions in butter; stir in flour. Drain mushrooms, reserving liquid. Add chicken broth to reserved mushroom liquid to make 1 1/2 cups liquid; stir into flour mixture gradually. Add cream; cook and stir until mixture thickens. Add rice, mushrooms, chicken, parsley, salt and pepper. Place in 2-quart casserole; sprinkle with almonds. Bake at 350 degrees for 30 minutes. Yield: 6 servings.

Jo Ann Vachule
The Fort Worth Star-Telegram

HOLIDAY CHICKEN CASSEROLE

4 c. soft bread, cubed
1/2 tsp. sage
1/8 tsp. pepper
1 tbsp. salt
1 c. chopped celery
2 minced onions, sauteed
4 to 5 c. cooked chicken
1/2 c. butter or chicken fat
1/3 c. flour
6 c. chicken broth
6 eggs, beaten
1 c. soft buttered crumbs

Mix bread cubes, sage, pepper, salt, celery and onions; place in 9 x 12-inch pan. Cut chicken in large pieces; place over bread mixture. Melt butter; blend in flour. Add broth; cook, stirring, until thickened. Add eggs; pour over chicken. Top with crumbs. Bake for 45 minutes at 350 degrees. Yield: 10 servings.

Dorothy Neighbors
The Seattle Times

Chicken-Tarragon En Casserole . . . poultry seasoned with delicious herbs

CHICKEN-TARRAGON EN CASSEROLE

1   5-lb. stewing hen
1 tbsp. dried tarragon
1 c. chopped fresh parsley
2 tsp. salt
1 lb. fine spaghetti or semolina
1/4 c. salad oil
1/2 lb. (or more) chicken livers
Flour seasoned with salt,
    pepper and paprika
1/2 c. finely chopped onion
1/4 c. finely chopped green pepper
1 tsp. hot paprika
2 c. shredded Cheddar cheese
1/2 c. dry white wine
1 lge. can pitted ripe olives, drained

Place hen in heavy kettle; cover with cold water. Add tarragon, parsley and salt; simmer for 4 to 5 hours or until tender. Remove chicken from broth. Strain broth; reserve. Remove chicken from bones; cut into small pieces. Set aside. Add water to reserved broth to make 1 gallon liquid; bring to a boil. Cook spaghetti in broth according to package directions; drain. Heat salad oil in large, heavy casserole. Dredge chicken livers with seasoned flour; saute in oil with onion and green pepper. Add paprika; stir to mix, breaking up livers as much as possible, making a coarse paste. Add chicken, spaghetti, cheese, wine and olives; mix

well. Bake in 300-degree oven until heated through and bubbling, about 30 minutes; add more wine if casserole is dry. Yield: 10-12 servings.

Jane Benet
The San Francisco Chronicle

SOUTH PACIFIC CHICKEN

Salt
1   3-lb. chicken, cut up
Flour
2 tbsp. sesame seed
1/2 c. sherry
2 tsp. brown sugar
2 tbsp. cooking oil
1 tbsp. soy sauce
1 tsp. ginger
1 can pineapple tidbits, drained
1 can water chestnuts, drained
Coconut (opt.)

Salt chicken; dredge in flour. Fry in oil until browned. Drain; roll in sesame seed. Place in baking dish. Mix sherry, sugar, 2 tablespoons oil, soy sauce, ginger, pineapple and sliced water chestnuts; pour over chicken. Cover. Bake for 45 minutes in 325-degree oven; sprinkle coconut over chicken before serving. Serve with rice and cooked oriental frozen vegetables. Yield: 6 servings.

Opal M. Crandall
The San Diego Union

SOUR CREAM CHICKEN

4 whole chicken breasts
1 c. sour cream
1 tbsp. Worcestershire sauce
1/2 tsp. red hot sauce
1 clove of garlic, pressed
1 1/2 tsp. paprika
2 tsp. salt
1 c. fine dry bread crumbs

Wash chicken breasts; dry. Make marinade of sour cream, Worcestershire sauce, red hot sauce and garlic; add seasonings. Add chicken; marinate overnight. Roll chicken in bread crumbs; place in single layer in large baking dish. Cover; chill for at least 1 hour and 30 minutes. Bake, uncovered, in 325-degree oven for 1 hour and 15 minutes. Yield: 4 servings.

Verna McCallum
The Indianapolis Star

TURKEY MARCO POLO

1 1/2 lb. broccoli
Butter or margarine
4 thin slices white turkey meat
4 thin slices cooked ham
2 tbsp. butter or margarine
Dash of cayenne
2 tbsp. grated Parmesan cheese
2 tbsp. shredded Swiss cheese
2 c. hot white sauce
1 tbsp. heavy cream, whipped

Cook broccoli according to package directions until just tender; drain thoroughly. Place in 4 individual shallow casseroles. Dot with butter; place 1 turkey slice on broccoli. Place ham slice on each turkey slice. Add 2 tablespoons butter, cayenne, Parmesan and Swiss cheeses to white sauce; stir until melted. Stir in whipped cream slowly; spoon over ham. Broil until glazed and bubbly. Yield: 4 servings.

Jeanne Voltz
The Los Angeles Times

GOURMET TURKEY CASSEROLE

1 1/2 c. sliced celery
1 med. onion, minced
1/2 c. butter or margarine
1/2 c. flour
Salt and pepper to taste
3 1/2 c. milk
1 can cream of mushroom soup, undiluted
2 c. cubed cooked ham
2 1/2 c. cubed cooked turkey
2 tbsp. minced pimento
1/4 tsp. dried basil
3 tbsp. sherry
1/2 c. grated Swiss cheese
Parsley sprigs

Saute celery and onion in butter until just tender. Stir in flour, salt, pepper and milk. Cook over medium heat, stirring constantly, until sauce is thickened. Add soup, ham, turkey, pimento, basil and sherry. Taste; add more seasonings, if needed. Turn into large casserole; top with cheese. Bake, uncovered, in 350-degree oven for 1 hour. Yield: 8 servings.

Julie Benell
The Dallas Morning News

SPAGHETTI WITH CLAM SAUCE

1 lb. thin spaghetti
3 cans minced clams and juice
1 lb. grated Swiss cheese
3 tbsp. dried chopped parsley
1 c. whipping cream
Salt and pepper to taste
1/4 to 1/2 c. grated Parmesan cheese

Cook spaghetti according to package directions. Drain; add remaining ingredients. Toss and serve. Add a light white sauce made with clam juice, if desired. Yield: 6-8 servings.

Jean Thwaite
The Atlanta Constitution

PEARS AND SHRIMP ORIENTAL

    1   1-lb. 13-oz. can pears
    2 tbsp. chopped onion
    2 tbsp. butter
    1 chicken bouillon cube
    1 med. green pepper, cut in strips
    2 tbsp. cornstarch
    1 tbsp. soy sauce
    2 tbsp. vinegar
    2   5-oz. cans shrimp, drained
    1/4 tsp. salt
    Dash of pepper
    1 can Chinese noodles

Drain pears; reserve syrup. Slice pear halves into quarters. Saute onion in butter for 3 minutes; add pears and continue to saute for 2 minutes longer. Dissolve bouillon cube in 3/4 cup hot pear syrup; add to pear and onion mixture. Add green pepper strips. Cover and bring to simmer. Mix cornstarch with 1/4 cup pear liquid; stir into pear mixture. Add soy sauce and vinegar. Cook until thickened. Add shrimp, salt and pepper. Heat through. Place noodles in bottom of baking dish. Pour pear mixture over top. Bake in 350-degree oven for 15 minutes. May be refrigerated before baking, then baked for 30 to 45 minutes. Yield: 4 servings.

Cyrilla Riley
The Detroit News

LOBSTER BAKED WITH MUSHROOMS

    3/4 lb. cooked lobster meat
    2 tbsp. chopped onion
    2 tbsp. chopped green pepper
    1   4-oz. can mushroom stems
        and pieces, drained
    2 tbsp. butter, melted
    3 tbsp. flour
    1/2 tsp. salt
    Dash of pepper
    1 1/2 c. milk

    1/2 c. grated cheese
    1 tbsp. butter, melted
    1/4 c. dry bread crumbs

Cut lobster meat into 1/2-inch pieces. Cook onion, green pepper and mushrooms in 2 tablespoons butter until tender. Blend in flour and seasonings. Add milk gradually; cook until thick, stirring constantly. Add cheese and lobster meat; heat. Place in 6 well-greased, individual 5-ounce custard cups. Combine 1 tablespoon butter and crumbs; sprinkle over top. Bake in 400-degree oven for 10 minutes or until brown. Yield: 6 servings.

Jane Benet
The San Francisco Chronicle

CHEESE AND BACON STRATA

    1/2 lb. bacon, cooked and crumbled
    1/2 c. thinly sliced celery
    1/4 c. chopped green pepper
    1/4 c. chopped onion
    8 slices day-old bread, trimmed
    4 slices Old English cheese
    4 eggs, beaten
    2 c. milk
    1 tsp. mustard
    1 tsp. salt
    Dash of pepper

Preheat oven to 325 degrees. Combine bacon, celery, green pepper and onion; mix until well blended. Arrange 4 slices bread in bottom of 8-inch square baking dish. Arrange bacon mixture on bread in baking dish. Place cheese slices on bacon mixture. Top with remaining bread. Combine eggs, milk, mustard and seasonings; blend well. Pour over sandwiches. Refrigerate for 1 hour. Bake in 375-degree oven for 1 hour or until puffy and brown. Yield: 4 servings.

Verna McCallum
The Indianapolis Star

Cheese Souffle ▶
. . . a masterpiece rich with cheese

BAKED GRITS

2 eggs, separated
2 c. cooked grits
1 c. milk
2 tbsp. butter
1/2 tsp. salt
4 drops of red hot sauce

Beat egg whites until soft but not stiff peaks form. Beat egg yolks, grits, milk and 1 tablespoon butter together until blended. Stir in egg whites, salt and red hot sauce. Pour into buttered 1-quart baking dish; top with remaining butter. Bake in 350-degree oven for 1 hour. Serve with Grillades. Yield: 4 servings.

Bettye Anding
The New Orleans States-Item

QUICK QUICHE

3 to 4 tbsp. imitation bacon bits
1 frozen pie crust, thawed
1 c. cheese, grated in blender
1 c. light cream
3 eggs
Salt to taste
White pepper to taste
1/2 tsp. nutmeg
Dash of cayenne pepper

Preheat oven to 350 degrees. Sprinkle bacon bits over pie crust. Top with cheese. Combine cream, eggs and seasonings in blender container; blend. Place pie dish on rack of oven. Pour egg mixture into crust. Bake for about 30 minutes or until mixture is set and golden brown on top. Cut into wedges; serve hot. Yield: 6 servings.

Dorothee Polson
The Arizona Republic

CHEESE SOUFFLE

Butter
5 slices bread
4 eggs, beaten
2 c. milk
1 tsp. prepared mustard
Salt to taste
1/2 lb. shredded Cheddar cheese

Preheat oven to 350 degrees. Spread butter on both sides bread; cut in quarters and arrange in casserole or baking dish. Combine eggs, milk, mustard, salt and cheese; pour over bread. Set casserole in pan of hot water. Bake for 50 minutes.

Patricia Williams
The Cincinnati Enquirer

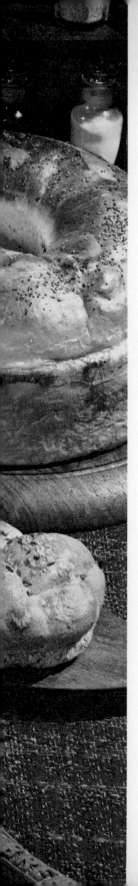

Old-Fashioned Homemade Biscuits, Buns, Rolls, Muffins, and Loaves

*B*ring *back the good old days and treat your family and friends to the best breads imaginable. Send the delicious aroma of tempting breads, muffins, or buns wafting from your kitchen.*

Bread making is one of the oldest of the culinary arts. People around the world have learned to bake their own special breads.

The art of baking is made easy with this collection of favorites. Each recipe contains clear instructions that assure success. America's most prominent food editors judged each recipe that follows to be a sure winner to complement any meal.

On the pages that follow, you will find such wonderful recipes as Hot Cross Buns, Crunchy Salad Biscuits, old fashioned White Bread, rich Sour Cream Rolls, southern Spoon Bread, delicious Maple Johnnycake, Hush Puppies, Cranberry Fruit-Nut Bread that is perfect for Christmas holidays, Orange Doughnuts the children will love and an unusual recipe for Bohemian Kolaches.

Breads

CRUNCHY SALAD BISCUITS

1 1/2 c. sifted flour
4 tsp. baking powder
1 tsp. salt
1/2 c. white hominy grits
1/4 c. shortening
1/4 c. chopped green onion
1 c. grated sharp cheese
1/2 c. (or more) milk
1 tbsp. grits

Sift flour, baking powder and salt together in bowl. Stir in 1/2 cup grits. Cut in shortening until mixture resembles coarse crumbs. Stir in onion and cheese. Add milk gradually, stirring lightly until just dampened. Add additional 1 tablespoon milk to make dough hold together if necessary. Form into ball. Turn out on lightly floured board; knead gently several times. Sprinkle board with 1 tablespoon grits. Roll dough to form 9 x 8-inch rectangle. Cut into eight 1-inch wide strips with sharp knife. Cut each strip into three 3-inch pieces. Place about 1 inch apart on ungreased cookie sheet. Bake at 425 degrees for 10 to 12 minutes or until lightly browned. Serve hot. Yield: 24 biscuits.

Julie Benell
The Dallas Morning News

WHOLE WHEAT BISCUITS

2 c. whole wheat flour
2 tsp. baking powder
1/4 tsp. salt
3 tbsp. shortening
1/2 c. milk

Sift dry ingredients; cut in shortening. Add milk and stir vigorously. Roll on lightly floured board to 1/2-inch thickness. Cut with biscuit cutter. Place on lightly greased cookie sheet. Bake for 10 minutes in 450-degree oven. Yield: 20 biscuits.

Jean Thwaite
The Atlanta Constitution

SOFT PRETZELS

1 c. warm water
3 pkg. dry yeast
3 c. flour
2 tsp. baking soda
1 egg
Coarse salt

Preheat oven to 400 degrees. Place warm water in large warm mixing bowl; sprinkle yeast over top, stirring until dissolved. Add flour gradually. Remove dough to lightly floured board. Knead for about 5 minutes. Shape into ball; place in bowl. Cover with dish towel. Let stand in warm dark place for about 30 minutes. Fill large shallow pan half full with water; add baking soda. Bring to a simmer. Punch dough down gently. Roll into 6-inch square. Cut into finger-sized strips with dull knife. Twist strips into pretzel shapes; pinch ends together. Slip pretzels, 1 at a time, into simmering water; let rise to surface. Remove with slotted spoon; place a few inches apart on greased cookie sheet. Beat egg with fork in small bowl. Brush pretzels with egg. Sprinkle with salt. Bake for about 15 minutes or until golden brown.

Elaine Tait
The Philadelphia Inquirer

WHITE BREAD

2 pkg. active dry yeast
1/2 c. lukewarm water
2 c. scalded milk
4 tbsp. shortening
3 tbsp. sugar
1 tbsp. salt
7 to 7 1/4 c. sifted flour

Sprinkle yeast over lukewarm water in cup; let stand for 5 minutes. Heat milk in saucepan until bubbly around edge of pan. Add shortening, sugar and salt, stirring until shortening is melted. Cool to lukewarm. Mix in 2 cups flour.

Hot Cross Buns . . . a seasonal special to enjoy year round

Stir in yeast. Add enough remaining flour to make dough easy to handle. Turn out onto floured board; knead for about 5 minutes or until dough is smooth and elastic. Place dough in large oiled bowl; oil top of dough. Cover with a damp cloth. Place bowl in unheated oven with pan of boiling water at side. Let rise for 1 hour and 30 minutes or until doubled in bulk. Punch down. Turn out on floured board; knead again. Divide dough in half; shape each into loaf. Place in oiled 9 x 5 x 3-inch bread pans; oil top. Cover. Let rise for about 1 hour or until doubled in bulk. Bake at 425 degrees for 25 to 30 minutes or until golden brown. Remove loaves immediately from pans onto racks. Do not place in direct draft. Yield: 2 loaves.

Alice Petersen
The New York News

HOT CROSS BUNS

2 pkg. dry yeast
1/4 c. warm water
2/3 c. scalded milk, cooled to
    lukewarm
1/3 c. sugar
3/4 tsp. salt
1/2 c. soft butter or margarine
3 eggs
4 c. (or more) sifted flour
2/3 c. currants
1/2 tsp. cinnamon
Oil
1 egg white, slightly beaten
Confectioners' sugar

Sprinkle yeast over warm water; let stand until dissolved. Pour lukewarm milk into large bowl; beat in sugar, salt, soft butter, eggs and 1 cup flour. Beat in yeast, currants and cinnamon; beat in remaining flour until dough is soft. Place in oiled bowl; brush top with oil. Cover with towel; let rise until doubled in bulk. Turn out on floured board; knead in small amount of flour if necessary. Roll dough out to 3/4-inch thickness; cut with 2-inch floured biscuit cutter. Shape into buns. Place on buttered baking sheet; brush buns with egg white. Let rise until puffy. Bake at 350 degrees until golden; remove to rack. Add enough confectioners' sugar to remaining egg white to make thick consistency; fashion a cross on each bun. Yield: 24 buns.

Alice Petersen
The New York News

Sour Cream Rolls

WHOLE WHEAT BREAD

3 c. warm water
3/4 c. (firmly packed) brown sugar
2 pkg. dry yeast
4 c. flour
4 tsp. salt
1/2 c. butter or margarine
1 c. hot water
8 c. whole wheat flour

Combine 1/2 cup warm water and 1/4 cup brown sugar; add yeast. Stir until dissolved. Add remaining water and brown sugar. Mix in 4 cups flour and salt; beat until smooth. Cover; let rise until doubled in bulk. Melt butter in hot water; cool. Punch dough down; add butter mixture and whole wheat flour. Mix well and knead for 10 minutes. Place dough in greased bowl; cover. Let rise until doubled in bulk. Punch down; shape into 3 loaves. Place in 3 buttered 9 x 5 x 3-inch loaf pans. Cover; let rise until doubled in bulk. Bake at 350 degrees for 40 to 45 minutes or until browned. Yield: 3 loaves.

Marjean Phillips Busby
The Kansas City Star and Times

SOUR CREAM ROLLS

1 pkg. dry or compressed yeast
1/2 c. lukewarm water
3/4 c. butter or margarine
2 eggs
1 c. sour cream
6 c. sifted flour
1 1/4 tsp. salt
1/2 c. sugar

Sprinkle yeast over lukewarm water to soften. Melt butter; cool. Beat eggs until thick; stir in melted butter, sour cream and yeast. Sift flour, salt and sugar together. Beat 1/2 of the flour mixture into egg mixture. Knead in remaining flour mixture. Place dough in greased bowl; let rise in warm spot until doubled in bulk. Punch down; shape into small balls. Place on greased baking sheet; let rise until doubled in bulk. Bake at 375 degrees for 10 to 15 minutes. Yield: 18 rolls.

Dorothy Neighbors
The Seattle Times

CHOCOLATE WAFFLE

1/2 c. butter
7/8 c. sugar
2 sq. melted chocolate
2 eggs
1/2 tsp. salt
1 1/2 c. flour
1/2 tsp. cinnamon
1/4 tsp. almond extract
1 tsp. vanilla

Cream butter and sugar; add chocolate. Blend in eggs and remaining ingredients. Pour into hot waffle iron; bake until done. Serve ice cream on waffles.

Elinor Lee
The Washington Post

EVIE'S POPOVERS

2 eggs
1 c. milk
1 c. all-purpose flour
1/2 tsp. salt

Combine eggs, milk, flour and salt in bowl; mix well, disregarding lumps. Fill greased muffin pans 3/4 full. Place in cold oven. Bake at 450 degrees for 30 minutes.

Verna McCallum Gall
The Indianapolis Star and News

JALAPENO CORN BREAD

1 c. cornmeal
2 tsp. baking powder
1 tsp. baking soda
1 tsp. salt
2 eggs
1 c. milk
1 1-lb. 1-oz. can cream-style corn
5 jalapeno peppers, finely chopped
1/4 c. bacon drippings
1/4 lb. grated sharp cheese

Combine cornmeal, baking powder, soda and salt. Beat eggs; mix with milk. Stir into dry ingredients. Add corn, peppers and bacon drippings. Pour half the mixture into greased 9-inch square pan. Sprinkle with cheese; cover with remaining batter. Bake at 350 degrees for 1 hour.

Jo Ann Vachule
The Fort Worth Star-Telegram

SPOON BREAD

1 c. white cornmeal
2 c. milk
1 tsp. sugar
1 tsp. salt
1 tbsp. butter
3 eggs, separated
2 tsp. baking powder

Cook cornmeal and milk together until a thick mush. Add sugar, salt and butter. Stir small amount of hot mixture into beaten egg yolks gradually; return egg yolks to hot mixture. Beat well. Add baking powder. Fold in beaten whites. Pour into 1 1/2-quart buttered baking dish. Bake for 20 minutes in

hot 400-degree oven. Serve immediately. Great with country ham and red-eye gravy. Yield: 6-8 servings.

Jean Thwaite
The Atlanta Constitution

Maple Johnnycake
. . . an early American favorite

OLD-FASHIONED MAPLE JOHNNYCAKE

1 1/3 c. sifted flour
3 tsp. baking powder
1/2 tsp. salt
2/3 c. yellow cornmeal
2 eggs, beaten
2/3 c. milk
1/3 c. maple syrup
1/3 c. melted shortening

Sift flour with baking powder and salt; add cornmeal. Combine eggs, milk, maple syrup and shortening; add to dry ingredients. Stir just enough to mix thoroughly; do not beat. Pour into greased 9 x 9-inch pan. Bake in 400-degree oven for about 30 minutes. Serve piping hot with butter. Yield: 9-12 muffins.

Beverly Kees
The Minneapolis Star

95

HUSH PUPPIES

1 c. fine white cornmeal
1 tbsp. flour
3/4 tsp. salt
1/2 tsp. white pepper
2 tsp. baking powder
1 med. onion, finely minced
1 egg
6 tbsp. evaporated milk
Cooking oil

Sift dry ingredients; add onion and egg. Beat well. Add milk; beat until smooth. Heat about 2 inches oil in electric skillet to 380 degrees. Drop enough batter from tablespoon to make about golf ball size into hot oil. Slide batter from side of spoon. Fry until golden brown. Remove with slotted spoon; drain. Serve hot. These crispy little balls are sometimes rolled in powdered sugar, but I like them plain. The absolute answer to a bread to accompany barbecue or any fish dish, whether stewed, broiled or fried. Yield: 4 servings.

Kay Jarvis
The San Diego Evening Tribune

COWBOY COFFEE CAKE

1 1/4 c. flour
1 c. brown sugar
1/4 tsp. salt
1/3 c. shortening
1 tsp. baking powder
1/4 tsp. baking soda
1/4 tsp. cinnamon
1/4 tsp. nutmeg
1/2 c. sour milk
1 egg, well beaten

Combine flour, sugar, salt and shortening; mix until crumbly. Reserve 1/3 cup for topping. Add baking powder, soda and spices to remaining sugar mixture; mix thoroughly. Add milk and egg; mix well. Pour into greased 8 x 8 x 2-inch baking pan; sprinkle with

reserved topping. Bake at 375 degrees for 25 to 30 minutes; serve warm.

Yvonne Rothert
The Oregonian

SOUR CREAM COFFEE CAKE

1/2 c. butter
1 c. sugar
2 eggs
1 tsp. vanilla
2 c. sifted all-purpose flour
1 tsp. baking powder
1 tsp. baking soda
1/2 tsp. salt
1 c. sour cream
1/3 c. chopped nuts
1/3 c. brown sugar
1 tsp. cinnamon

Preheat oven to 350 degrees. Cream butter and sugar together until fluffy; beat in eggs and vanilla. Sift flour, baking powder, soda and salt together; add to butter mixture alternately with sour cream. Combine remaining ingredients for topping. Spoon half the batter into greased 10-inch tube pan; sprinkle with half the topping. Add remaining batter; add remaining topping. Bake for 45 minutes; do not open oven while baking. Cool; turn out of pan. Drizzle with confectioners' sugar icing, if desired; garnish with walnut halves. This recipe came from Mrs. Stephen Beach, member of Western Reserve Herb Society, a group noted for fine flavorful cooking, much of it with homegrown herbs.

Janet Beighle
The Cleveland Plain Dealer

GLAZED ORANGE ROLLS

1 c. orange juice, heated
1/4 c. butter or margarine
1/2 c. (firmly packed) brown sugar
1 1/2 tsp. salt
1/2 c. cold water

Cranberry Fruit-Nut Bread . . . festive holiday loaf

4 1/4 to 4 3/4 c. sifted
    all-purpose flour
2 eggs
2 pkg. dry yeast
1 c. quick or old-fashioned oats
2 tsp. grated orange peel
Melted shortening
Melted butter
1/2 c. honey
Grated peel of 1 orange

Combine orange juice, butter, sugar and salt; stir to melt butter. Add water; cool to lukewarm. Add 2 cups flour, eggs and yeast; beat until smooth, about 2 minutes. Add oats, 2 teaspoons orange peel and enough remaining flour to make soft dough. Knead on lightly floured board or canvas until smooth and satiny, about 10 minutes. Form into ball; place in greased bowl. Brush with shortening. Cover; let rise in warm place until doubled in bulk, about 1 hour. Punch down. Shape into 24 rolls; place in greased medium-sized muffin cups. Brush with melted butter; cover. Let rise in warm place until nearly doubled in bulk, about 45 minutes. Bake in moderate 375-degree oven for 12 to 15 minutes. Combine honey and grated peel of 1 orange; brush on warm rolls.

Carol Voshall
The Phoenix Gazette

CRANBERRY FRUIT-NUT BREAD

2 c. all-purpose flour, sifted
1 c. sugar
1 1/2 tsp. baking powder
1/2 tsp. baking soda
1 tsp. salt
1/4 c. shortening
3/4 c. orange juice
1 tbsp. grated orange rind
1 egg, well beaten
1/2 c. chopped nuts
1 to 2 c. fresh or frozen cranberries

Sift flour, sugar, baking powder, soda and salt together; cut in shortening until mixture resembles coarse cornmeal. Combine orange juice and grated rind with egg. Pour all at once into flour mixture; mix just enough to dampen ingredients. Fold in nuts and coarsely chopped cranberries. Spoon into greased 9 x 5 x 3-inch loaf pan. Spread corners and sides slightly higher than center. Bake in moderate 350-degree oven for about 1 hour or until crust is golden brown and inserted toothpick comes out clean. Remove from pan; cool. Store overnight for easy slicing. Do not thaw frozen cranberries. Rinse quickly in cold water; chop while frozen.

Janet Christensen
The Boston Herald Traveler

ORANGE DOUGHNUTS

1 c. sugar
3 eggs, well beaten
2 tbsp. grated orange rind
2 tbsp. melted butter
3/4 c. buttermilk
1/4 c. orange juice
4 1/2 c. sifted all-purpose flour
1 tsp. soda
2 tsp. baking powder
1 tsp. salt
Fat
Icing or sugar coating (opt.)

Beat sugar into eggs gradually; add orange rind, butter, buttermilk and orange juice. Sift flour with soda, baking powder and salt; add to sugar mixture gradually. Mix well; chill for 2 hours. Divide dough in half; roll each part 1/3 inch thick on well-floured pastry cloth. Cut with 3-inch doughnut cutter. Fry in hot fat at 360 degrees for about 3 minutes, turning doughnuts as they rise to surface and brown. Drain on paper toweling; add icing. Best served day prepared. Yield: 2 1/2 dozen.

Ruth Ellen Church
The Chicago Tribune

GOOEY BUTTER CAKE

1/4 c. milk
1/4 c. water
1/2 stick soft butter or margarine
1 pkg. dry yeast
2 1/2 to 2 3/4 c. all-purpose flour
1/4 c. sugar
1/2 tsp. salt
1 egg

Heat milk, water and butter over low heat until warm; butter does not have to melt. Cool to lukewarm. Mix yeast with 3/4 cup flour, sugar and salt in large mixer bowl; add milk mixture. Beat at medium speed for 2 minutes, scraping bowl occasionally. Add about 1/4 cup flour or enough to make thick batter; add egg. Beat at high speed for 2 minutes or with spoon for 6 minutes, scraping bowl occasionally. Remove beaters; stir in enough flour to make thick but not sticky dough. Turn out onto floured board; work in just enough flour to handle easily. Knead for about 5 minutes or until smooth and elastic; divide in half. Place in 2 greased and floured 8-inch square pans; press as thin as possible and up around edges of pans. Let rise while preparing Filling. Preheat oven to 350 degrees.

FILLING

2 sticks butter
1/2 c. shortening
3/4 c. sweetened condensed milk
3/4 c. white corn syrup
2 eggs
3/4 c. all-purpose flour
1 1/2 tsp. vanilla
Pinch of salt

Cream butter and shortening together until fluffy. Add 1/2 cup milk; beat until light. Add syrup; mix thoroughly. Add eggs, 1 at a time; mix thoroughly. Add flour to creamed mixture alternately with remaining milk. Add vanilla and salt; mix well. Pour over dough in pans. Bake for about 30 minutes; cool. Filling will set after cooling.

Marian O'Brien
The St. Louis Globe-Democrat

ORANGE BOWS

1 1/4 c. scalded milk
1/2 c. shortening
1/3 c. sugar
1 tsp. salt
1 cake or 1 pkg. yeast
2 eggs, beaten
1/2 c. orange juice
2 tbsp. grated orange peel
5 c. (about) all-purpose flour
2 tbsp. orange juice

1 tsp. grated orange peel
1 c. powdered sugar

Combine milk, shortening, sugar and salt; cool to lukewarm. Soften yeast in milk mixture; add eggs, 1/2 cup orange juice and grated peel. Beat well; beat in flour gradually. Knead until smooth and satiny. Place in greased bowl; cover. Let rise until doubled in bulk; punch down. Roll out on lightly floured board; cut in strips about 8 inches long. Roll each strip lightly; tie in loose knot. Arrange on greased baking sheets; tuck ends under. Let rise until almost doubled in bulk. Bake in 400-degree oven for 12 minutes or until done. Mix remaining ingredients; spread on hot buns. May be made smaller for delicious dainty roll.

Marjorie Anderson "Mary Cullen"
The Oregon Journal

BOHEMIAN KOLACHES

1/2 c. milk
2 pkg. dry yeast
1/2 c. warm water
3/4 c. butter
1/2 c. sugar
1 tsp. salt
4 egg yolks
4 1/2 c. sifted all-purpose flour
Prune-Apricot Filling
2 tbsp. melted butter
2 tbsp. powdered sugar

Scald milk; cool to lukewarm. Sprinkle yeast on water; stir to dissolve. Cream butter, sugar, salt and egg yolks with electric mixer until light and fluffy. Add yeast, milk and 1 1/2 cups flour; beat with electric mixer at medium speed for 5 minutes, scraping bowl occasionally. Stir in remaining flour, small amount at a time, to make soft dough. Place in lightly greased bowl; turn to grease top. Cover; let rise in warm place, free from drafts, until doubled in bulk, about 1 hour to 1 hour and 30 minutes. Stir down; turn onto lightly floured board. Divide into 24 equal pieces; shape each piece into ball. Cover; let rest for 10 to 15 minutes. Place 2 inches apart on greased baking sheets; press each piece from center outward with fingers to make hollow center with 1/2-inch rim. Fill each hollow with 1 tablespoon Prune-Apricot Filling. Cover; let rise in warm place until doubled in bulk, 30 to 40 minutes. Bake at 350 degrees for 15 to 18 minutes or until browned. Brush lightly with melted butter; sprinkle lightly with powdered sugar. Remove from baking sheets; place on wire racks. Yield: 24 kolaches.

PRUNE-APRICOT FILLING

1 c. prunes
3/4 c. dried apricots
1/2 c. sugar
1 tbsp. orange juice
1 tbsp. grated orange peel

Simmer prunes and apricots in water to cover until tender; drain. Chop; mash with fork. Stir in sugar, orange juice and grated peel; mixture should be thick. Yield: Filling for 24 kolaches.

Eleanor Ostman
The St. Paul Dispatch-Pioneer Press

WHIPPED BUTTER

1/2 lb. butter
1/2 lb. sugar
1/2 doz. macaroons, crumbled
Grated peel of 2 oranges
1 doz. blanched almonds, finely
  chopped
1 oz. brandy or Cointreau

Cream butter and sugar; add remaining ingredients in order listed and blend to a smooth paste. Serve with toasted rolls, English muffin halves or toast. This delectable concoction adds a Midas touch to brunch or breakfast.

Elinor Lee
The Washington Post

Delicious Dishes of Savory Sweetness
to Top off Any Great Meal

T o many people – especially young people of all
ages – the dessert course is the highpoint of
a meal. It is the crowning touch of sweetness that
tops the main course, and brings satisfaction and
contentment around the table.

Desserts come in a wide variety. Some are served
hot, some at room temperature, and others are chilled
or frozen. The number of desserts is practically
endless, but the leading newspaper editors of America
have selected the ones that follow as the most delectable of all the eye-appealing, taste-tempting dessert
recipes which they have encountered in their years
of professional experience.

Here you will find such supreme concoctions as Blackberry
Jam Cake, a Peerless Carrot Cake, rich Chocolate Velvet
Cake, Fort Worth's Favorite Fruitcake, Easy Rocky
Road Candy, South Kentucky Fudge, New Orleans Pralines,
a Frozen Plum Pudding, beautiful Pears de Cacao, Chocolate
Vienna Torte and a Superb Black Bottom Pie.

Desserts

BLACKBERRY JAM CAKE

1 1/2 c. sugar
3/4 c. butter or margarine
3 egg yolks, beaten
1 1/2 c. blackberry jam
2 tbsp. cocoa
2 1/2 c. flour
1/2 tsp. cinnamon
1/2 tsp. nutmeg
1/2 tsp. cloves
3/4 c. buttermilk
1 1/2 tsp. baking soda
1 tsp. milk
3 egg whites, slightly beaten

Cream sugar and butter until fluffy. Add egg yolks; beat well. Stir in jam. Dissolve cocoa in small amount of water; stir into sugar mixture. Sift flour and spices together; add to sugar mixture alternately with buttermilk, beating well after each addition. Dissolve soda in milk; add to cake mixture. Beat well; beat in egg whites. Pour into well-oiled tube pan or 2 greased and lightly floured cake pans. Bake at 350 degrees for 1 hour to 1 hour and 10 minutes.

Bertha Scott
The Indianapolis News

PEERLESS CARROT CAKE

2 2/3 c. sugar or brown sugar
2 2/3 c. water
1 tsp. allspice
1 tsp. cloves
1 tsp. cinnamon
2 tbsp. butter
2 c. finely grated carrots
2 c. seedless raisins
4 c. flour
3 tsp. baking soda
2 c. chopped walnuts

Boil sugar, water, spices, butter, carrots and raisins together for 20 minutes. Remove from heat; stir in 2/3 cup cold water. Cool. Sift flour and soda together; stir into carrot mixture. Add walnuts; mix well. Pour into oiled

and floured large tube pan. Bake for 1 hour at 350 degrees. Recipe goes back to my great grandmother's day. May be stored in aluminum foil for weeks in refrigerator. May be served with hard sauce, ice cream, whipped cream or tart lemon icing. Yield: 12-15 servings.

Kay Jarvis
The San Diego Evening Tribune

MOTHER'S CHOCOLATE SPICE CAKE

1 1/2 c. sugar
2 c. cake flour
1 tsp. salt
1 tsp. baking powder
1/2 tsp. baking soda
1 tsp. cloves
1 tsp. cinnamon
1 tsp. nutmeg
1 c. milk
1/2 c. butter
2 1-oz. sq. unsweetened chocolate
2/3 c. eggs
1/4 tsp. red food coloring

Sift sugar, flour, salt, baking powder, soda, cloves, cinnamon and nutmeg together into large mixing bowl. Add 2/3 cup milk and butter; beat for 2 minutes. Add melted chocolate and eggs; beat for 2 minutes. Add remaining milk and red coloring; beat for 1 minute. Spread batter into 2 greased and floured 9-inch round cake pans. Bake at 350 degrees for 35 minutes; cool. Frost with seven-minute frosting. Combines old-fashioned goodness of spices and chocolate. Yield: 12-16 servings.

Marjorie Anderson "Mary Cullen"
The Oregon Journal

CHOCOLATE VELVET CAKE

1 6-oz. pkg. semisweet chocolate morsels
1/4 c. water
2 1/4 c. sifted cake flour

1 tsp. baking soda
3/4 tsp. salt
1 3/4 c. sugar
3/4 c. softened butter
1 tsp. vanilla
3 eggs, at room temperature
1 c. water

Combine chocolate morsels and 1/4 cup water in saucepan; cook and stir over low heat until melted and smooth. Remove from heat. Sift flour, baking soda and salt together; set aside. Combine sugar, butter and vanilla in bowl; beat until well blended. Add eggs, one at a time, beating well after each addition. Blend in melted chocolate mixture; stir in flour mixture alternately with 1 cup water. Pour into 2 greased and floured 9-inch round pans. Bake at 375 degrees for 30 to 35 minutes. Cool.

CHOCOLATE VELVET FROSTING

1 6-oz. pkg. semisweet chocolate
   morsels
3 tbsp. butter or margarine
1/4 c. milk
1 tsp. vanilla
1/4 tsp. salt
3 c. sifted confectioners' sugar

Melt chocolate morsels and butter in saucepan over hot, not boiling, water. Remove from water. Add milk, vanilla and salt; mix until well blended. Beat in confectioners' sugar gradually. Fill and frost cake.

Elaine Tait
The Philadelphia Inquirer

GRACE'S COCONUT CAKE

1 c. butter
2 c. sugar
4 eggs, separated
3 tsp. baking powder
3 c. flour
1 c. milk
1/2 tsp. lemon extract
1/2 tsp. vanilla

Chocolate Velvet Cake

Cream butter, sugar and egg yolks together. Sift baking powder with flour; add to creamed mixture alternately with milk. Add flavorings and stiffly beaten egg whites; pour into three 9-inch layer pans. Bake at 350 degrees for about 25 minutes or until done. Cool.

FILLING

3 eggs
1 1/2 c. sugar
1 c. milk
2 1/2 c. flaked or shredded coconut
1 tsp. vanilla

Beat eggs; add sugar, milk and coconut. Cook, stirring constantly, to custard consistency. Stir in vanilla; cool. Spread between layers and on top of cake; sprinkle with additional coconut, if desired.

Grace Hartley
The Atlanta Journal

FORT WORTH'S FAVORITE FRUITCAKE

1 lb. pitted dates
1/2 lb. candied cherries
1/2 lb. candied sliced pineapple
1 lb. coarsely chopped pecans
1 c. sugar
1 c. flour
2 tsp. baking powder
1/2 tsp. salt
1 tsp. nutmeg
4 eggs
1 tsp. vanilla

Line angel food tube pan with heavy brown paper. Cut fruits into small pieces; mix with pecans. Sift dry ingredients together; mix with fruits and nuts. Beat eggs with vanilla; pour over fruit mixture. Mix well. Pack into pan. Bake for 2 hours at 250 degrees. Top of fruitcake may be decorated by removing cake from oven after 1 hour, garnishing with pineapple slices, halved cherries and pecan halves; return to oven to complete baking time.

Jo Ann Vachule
The Fort Worth Star-Telegram

FRUIT COCKTAIL CAKE

4 tbsp. shortening
2 tbsp. flour
1 1-lb. can fruit cocktail and juice
2 c. sugar
3 eggs
3 c. sifted flour
3 tsp. baking soda
1 tsp. salt
1 tsp. cinnamon
1 1/2 c. chopped walnuts or pecans
1 1/2 c. raisins
2 tbsp. cognac or rum

Grease 8-inch tube pan with mixture of 4 tablespoons shortening and 2 tablespoons flour. Place next 10 ingredients in large bowl. Stir until well blended. Pour into prepared tube pan. Bake in moderately slow 325-degree oven for 2 hours or until cake tester inserted in center comes out clean. Set on rack; let stand for 5 minutes. Run small spatula around tube and side of pan; turn out on rack. Cool.

BUTTER SAUCE

1/2 c. butter
3/4 c. sugar
1/2 c. evaporated milk
2 tbsp. cognac or rum
Candied cherries
Flaked coconut

Boil butter, sugar and evaporated milk in saucepan for 3 minutes. Add cognac. Spoon hot sauce over cake. Garnish with candied cherries and coconut. Serve in wedges. Yield: 8 servings.

Alice Petersen
The New York News

PRIZE MOCHA PRUNE CAKE

1/2 c. shortening
1 1/2 c. sugar
3 lge. eggs, well beaten
2 c. all-purpose flour
1/2 tsp. salt
1 tsp. baking soda
1 tsp. baking powder
1 tsp. cinnamon
1 tsp. nutmeg
1 tsp. allspice
1 c. buttermilk
1 c. chopped prunes, well drained
Mocha Icing

Cream shortening; add sugar. Add eggs; beat until smooth. Add sifted dry ingredients alternately with buttermilk; cut in prunes. Place in 3 greased 8-inch layer cake pans. Bake at 350 degrees for 25 to 30 minutes; cool. Fill and frost with Mocha Icing.

MOCHA ICING

6 tbsp. shortening or butter
1 egg yolk, beaten
3 c. sifted confectioners' sugar
1 1/2 tbsp. cocoa
5 tbsp. hot strong coffee

Cream shortening. Add egg yolk; blend. Combine sugar with cocoa; add to egg yolk mixture alternately with coffee.

Margaret C. Bowers
The Oakland Tribune

CONFECTIONERS' SUGAR POUND CAKE

1 lb. butter
6 eggs
1 lb. confectioners' sugar
1 1/2 tsp. vanilla
3 c. sifted flour

Have butter and eggs at room temperature. Cream butter well; beat in sugar gradually until light and fluffy. Beat in eggs, one at a time, beating well after each addition. Add vanilla; beat in flour gradually. Mix to silky consistency; pour into well-greased 9 or 10-inch tube pan. Bake at 325 degrees for 1 hour or until cake springs back when touched. Cool in pan for 10 minutes. Shake loose in pan; turn out on rack to cool. Store in tightly covered tin or wrap well in waxed paper or aluminum foil.

Ella Elvin
The New York News

SAM HOUSTON WHITE CAKE

3/4 c. butter or margarine
2 c. sugar
3 c. sifted flour
3 tsp. baking powder
1/2 tsp. salt
1 tsp. vanilla
1/2 tsp. almond flavoring
1/2 c. milk
1/2 c. water
6 egg whites
Shiny Chocolate Frosting

Cream butter until soft and light. Add sugar gradually; cream for several minutes longer. Combine flour, baking powder and salt; sift 3 times. Mix flavorings, milk and water; add to creamed mixture alternately with flour mixture, beating well after each addition. Beat egg whites until stiff, but not dry; fold into cake mixture. Blend well; do not beat. Pour into 3 greased and floured 9-inch layer pans. Bake at 350 degrees for 25 minutes; cool for 5 minutes. Turn onto racks; remove pans. Cool; frost with Shiny Chocolate Frosting.

SHINY CHOCOLATE FROSTING

3 1-oz. sq. unsweetened chocolate
2 c. sifted powdered sugar
1/8 tsp. salt
1/4 c. hot water
3 egg yolks
1/4 c. melted butter
1 tsp. vanilla

Melt chocolate over hot water. Remove from heat; stir in powdered sugar, salt and water. Beat in egg yolks, one at a time, beating well after each addition. Add butter, a small amount at a time; add vanilla. This is an heirloom recipe favorite of early Texas.

Ann M. Criswell
The Houston Chronicle

RUM CAKE

1/2 c. water
1 c. sugar
1 tbsp. rum or rum extract
1/2 c. margarine
1 3/4 c. sugar
5 eggs
2 c. flour
1 tsp. vanilla

Bring water and 1 cup sugar to a boil; boil for 1 minute. Cool. Add rum. Cream margarine. Add 1 3/4 cups sugar; beat until fluffy. Add eggs, one at a time, alternately with flour; add vanilla. Place in greased tube pan. Bake for 1 hour at 325 degrees. Pour rum sauce over warm cake.

Grace Hartley
The Atlanta Journal

FREEZER FROSTING

1 2/3 c. sugar
1/2 c. water
1/4 tsp. cream of tartar
1/2 c. egg whites
1/2 tsp. vanilla

Boil sugar, water and cream of tartar to 260 degrees on candy thermometer. Beat whites until stiff; add sugar mixture slowly. Add vanilla. Beat until frosting holds shape. Freezes well. Yield: Frosting for two 9-inch layers.

Mary Hart
The Minneapolis Tribune

POTATO FONDANT

4 oz. mashed potatoes
12 oz. powdered sugar
4 oz. coconut
1 tsp. vanilla
Melted chocolate

Mix first 4 ingredients; chill for several hours. Knead with hands until smooth and creamy. Shape into bonbons; dip in melted chocolate. May be tinted with food coloring, if desired. May use rum, lemon, maple or any other extract instead of vanilla. Mashed potatoes must be free of lumps to give candy smooth, satiny texture. The recipe is so old the source is unknown. It was given to me by my grandmother. She always served the fondant in frilly, little paper cups. Yield: 1 1/2 pounds.

Kay Jarvis
The San Diego Evening Tribune

EASY ROCKY ROAD

1/2 lb. marshmallows
1 c. broken walnuts
1 lb. milk chocolate

Sprinkle marshmallows and walnuts in oiled 9-inch square pan. Melt chocolate in top of double boiler over warm water; do not let chocolate get more than lukewarm. Melting process takes about 30 minutes. Pour chocolate over marshmallow mixture; cool until thick and firm. Cut into squares. Yield: 81 pieces.

Dorothy Neighbors
The Seattle Times

PINEAPPLE WHITE FUDGE

2 c. sugar
1/2 c. sour cream
1/3 c. white corn syrup
2 tbsp. butter
1/4 tsp. salt
1 tsp. vanilla
3/4 c. natural, red and green
    candied pineapple
1/2 c. chopped nuts

Combine sugar, sour cream, corn syrup, butter and salt; bring to a boil over medium heat, stirring, until sugar dissolves. Boil, without stirring, to 236 degrees on candy thermometer or until small amount dropped in cold water forms soft ball. Add vanilla; beat until mixture starts to lose gloss, about 8 minutes. Stir in pineapple and nuts; pour into buttered 8-inch square pan. Cool; cut into squares.

Eleanor Ostman
The St. Paul Dispatch-Pioneer Press

SOUTH KENTUCKY FUDGE

1 c. buttermilk or sour cream
1 tsp. baking soda
2 c. sugar
2 tbsp. butter
1 tsp. vanilla

Combine buttermilk and baking soda in 1-quart heavy saucepan; let stand for 5 minutes. Stir in sugar gradually; cook over medium heat, stirring, until completely dissolved. Place candy thermometer in saucepan. Add butter and vanilla; cook, stirring occasionally, to 232 degrees on thermometer or to soft-ball stage. Remove from heat; cool, without shaking or stirring, until just warmer than room temperature, about 100 degrees. Beat until candy loses gloss and begins to hold shape. Pour out on buttered plate; cut in squares immediately. Candy foams very much during cooking; turns from white to light caramel color. Do not double recipe. Yield: 1 pound.

Lillian Marshall
The Louisville Courier-Journal

MARZIPAN CANDY

1 1/4 lb. pure almond paste
3 tbsp. light corn syrup
1 lb. powdered sugar
1 tbsp. marshmallow creme
Pinch of salt
Color pastes

Place all ingredients except color pastes in bowl; knead with hands for about 10 minutes or until consistency of heavy pie dough. Break off small pieces; color desired shades. Shape as desired.

Opal M. Crandall
The San Diego Union

SHOE BOX PEANUT BRITTLE

2 c. salted peanuts
1 1/2 c. sugar
1 1/2 c. light corn syrup
1/4 c. water
2 tbsp. butter
1 tsp. baking soda
1/2 tsp. vanilla
2 tsp. cold water

Place peanuts in shallow pan. Bake at 275 degrees until heated through. Combine sugar, syrup and 1/4 cup water in 2-quart heavy saucepan; cook over high heat, stirring with wooden spoon, until sugar is completely dissolved. Wipe sugar crystals from side of pan with wet cloth; cook, without stirring, to 275 degrees on candy thermometer. Remove thermometer; lower heat to medium. Add butter and hot peanuts; cook, stirring constantly, for 5 minutes. Place thermometer back in candy; cook, stirring, to 300 degrees on thermometer. Remove from heat; stir in mixture of baking soda, vanilla and cold water. Stir hard for 30 seconds; candy will foam. Pour out on buttered marble slab; spread quickly with spatula. Stretch brittle thin by grasping edges and pulling gently when edges have cooled enough to handle. Break into pieces when cold. Recipe just about fills small-sized shoe box for mailing.

Lillian Marshall
The Louisville Courier-Journal

NEW ORLEANS PRALINES

4 tbsp. water
2 tbsp. cream or evaporated milk
1 tbsp. butter
1/2 tsp. salt
4 c. brown sugar
2 c. broken pecans
3/4 tbsp. sherry

Combine water, cream, butter, salt and brown sugar in heavy saucepan; melt over very low heat. Bring to a boil gradually, stirring constantly; add pecans and sherry. Cook until candy begins to thicken; remove from heat. Stir while cooling. Drop from large spoon onto waxed paper while still pourable, making 3 or 4-inch cakes. Recipe was given to me by Edgar T. (Scoop) Gleeson, legendary San Francisco newspaperman, now retired. He notes that you may use a dozen drops of vanilla in place of sherry; he uses Spanish sherry, holding it out to the last so it doesn't lose all its bouquet.

Helen Civelli Brown
The San Francisco Examiner

BILL'S FAVORITE CHEESECAKE

18 zwieback
1/4 c. melted butter or margarine
2 tbsp. sugar
1 lb. cream cheese
1/2 c. sugar
1 tsp. vanilla
1 tsp. grated lemon rind
2 tbsp. lemon juice
3 eggs, separated
1 c. sour cream
1 tbsp. sugar
1 tsp. vanilla

Roll zwieback fine; mix with butter and 2 tablespoons sugar. Press in 9-inch springform pan. Blend cream cheese with 1/2 cup sugar, vanilla, lemon rind and lemon juice; add egg yolks, one at a time, beating well after each addition. Fold in stiffly beaten egg whites; pour on crumb crust. Bake at 300 degrees for 50 minutes. Mix remaining ingredients; spread on baked cheesecake. Bake for 10 minutes longer; cool before removing springform sides. Garnish with additional zwieback crumbs and maraschino cherry flowers. Yield: 8-10 servings.

Lillian Marshall
The Louisville Courier-Journal

LINDY'S CHEESECAKE

1 c. sifted all-purpose flour
1/4 c. sugar
1 tsp. grated lemon rind
Pulp from sm. piece of vanilla bean
1 egg yolk
1/2 c. soft butter
1 to 2 tbsp. water

Combine flour, sugar, lemon rind and vanilla pulp. Make well in center; add egg yolk and butter. Mix with hand until well blended, adding small amount of water at a time, if needed, to make light dough. Wrap in waxed paper; chill for about 1 hour. Roll out 1/8 inch thick; place over oiled bottom of 9-inch springform pan. Trim off dough by running rolling pin over sharp edge. Bake at 400 degrees for about 15 minutes or until golden; cool. Butter sides of pan; place over base. Roll out remaining dough 1/8 inch thick; cut band to fit sides of pan. Line sides of pan, pressing firmly against bottom crust.

FILLING

2 1/2 lb. cream cheese
1 3/4 c. sugar
3 tbsp. all-purpose flour
1 1/2 tsp. grated orange rind
1 1/2 tsp. grated lemon rind
1/4 tsp. vanilla
5 eggs
2 egg yolks
1/4 c. coffee cream
Strawberries or whipped cream

Beat cream cheese, sugar, flour, orange rind, lemon rind and vanilla together; blend thoroughly. Beat in eggs and egg yolks, one at a time, beating lightly after each addition. Fold in cream; pour into prepared pan. Bake at 500 degrees for 12 minutes. Reduce temperature to 200 degrees; bake for 1 hour longer. Turn off heat; let stand in oven for 15 minutes. Remove from oven; cool. Top with strawberries just before serving.

Marian O'Brien
The St. Louis Globe-Democrat

SISTER GEORGINA'S CHEESECAKE

2 tbsp. butter
2 tbsp. sugar
1 1/2 c. fine zwieback crumbs
2 8-oz. pkg. cream cheese
1 c. sugar
5 egg yolks
2 c. thick sour cream
1 tsp. vanilla
1 tsp. lemon juice
5 egg whites, beaten stiff

3 c. strawberries
1 c. sugar
3 tbsp. cornstarch
1 c. whole strawberries

Cream butter. Add 2 tablespoons sugar and crumbs; blend. Press in 9-inch springform pan. Have cream cheese at room temperature. Mash cream cheese. Add 1 cup sugar; blend. Add egg yolks, sour cream, vanilla and lemon juice; blend. Fold in egg whites; pour over crumb mixture. Bake at 300 degrees for 1 hour. Turn off heat; let cake remain in oven for 1 hour with door closed. Open door; leave cake in oven for 30 minutes longer. Chill for several hours or overnight. Remove sides of springform pan. Combine 3 cups strawberries, 1 cup sugar and 1 cup water; bring to a boil. Simmer for 15 minutes. Blend cornstarch with 1/3 cup water; stir into strawberry mixture. Cook, stirring constantly, until thick and clear. Strain; chill. Arrange whole strawberries on cheesecake; pour glaze over top, being sure to coat each strawberry. Sister Georgina is of Italian heritage; she is with a Dominican convent and prepares meals 3 times a day for sisters who teach at Lacordaire School in Upper Montclair, New Jersey.

Joan Babbage
The Newark Evening News

FORGOTTEN KISSES

2 egg whites
1/8 tsp. salt
1/2 tsp. cream of tartar
3/4 c. sugar
1/2 tsp. vanilla
1 6-oz. pkg. chocolate chips or
   chocolate shot

Preheat oven to 350 degrees. Beat egg whites until fluffy. Add salt and cream of tartar; beat. Add sugar slowly, beating constantly. Beat until glossy; add vanilla. Fold in chocolate chips. Drop from teaspoon onto greased cookie sheet. Place in moderate 350-degree oven; turn heat off immediately. Leave in oven at least 2 hours or until cool. Remove from oven and pan. Bake the night before in retained heat for afternoon tea. Yield: 4 dozen.

Marjorie Anderson "Mary Cullen"
The Oregon Journal

Sugar Cookies . . . an unusual recipe

SUGAR COOKIES

1 c. butter or margarine
3 c. sifted all-purpose flour
1/2 tsp. baking soda
2 eggs
1 tsp. vanilla
1 c. sugar

Cut butter into flour sifted with soda as for pie crust. Beat eggs and vanilla until thick and lemon colored. Beat in sugar gradually. Combine flour mixture and egg mixture; mix well. Chill for 3 hours or longer. Roll 1/3 of the dough at a time on floured pastry cloth to 1/4 to 1/8-inch thickness. Cut into rounds. Place on ungreased cookie sheets; sprinkle with additional sugar. Bake at 375 degrees for 8 to 10 minutes or until lightly browned. Yield: About 2 dozen cookies.

Ruth Ellen Church
The Chicago Tribune

SUGAR-TOPPED RAISIN BARS

1 egg
2/3 c. (packed) brown sugar
1/3 c. salad oil
1 tsp. vanilla
1 c. all-purpose flour
1/2 tsp. baking powder
1/4 tsp. salt
3/4 c. golden raisins
2 tbsp. sugar
1/2 tsp. cinnamon

Beat egg lightly; stir in brown sugar, oil and vanilla. Add sifted dry ingredients; blend well. Stir in raisins. Spread in greased 9 x 9-inch pan. Combine sugar and cinnamon; sprinkle over top. Bake at 350 degrees for about 25 minutes. Cool; cut into bars. Yield: About 24 bars.

Yvonne Rothert
The Oregonian

ETHEL'S FRUIT COOKIES

3 egg whites
1/2 c. sugar
1/2 c. flour
1 lb. dates, chopped
3 slices candied pineapple, chopped
2 c. pecans, chopped
1 tsp. vanilla

Beat egg whites until stiff; gradually add sugar, flour, fruits and pecans. Stir in vanilla. Drop by teaspoonfuls onto greased, foil-lined baking sheet. Bake for about 40 minutes at 275 degrees.

Jo Ann Vachule
The Fort Worth Star-Telegram

ALMOND-CHERRY BALLS

1 1/2 sticks butter
1/4 c. powdered sugar
2 c. sifted flour
1 c. ground almonds
1/4 tsp. salt
1 tsp. vanilla
Glazed whole cherries

Cream butter until light and fluffy. Blend in powdered sugar. Add flour, almonds, salt and vanilla. Stir until dough is thoroughly blended. Roll 1 teaspoon dough into ball around cherry. Bake in 325-degree oven for 20 minutes. Cool slightly; roll in additional powdered sugar. Yield: About 40 cookies.

Elaine Tait
The Philadelphia Inquirer

FATTIGMAND

6 egg yolks
6 tbsp. sugar
1 tbsp. melted butter
1/8 tsp. salt
6 tbsp. cream
2 c. (about) flour
1/4 tsp. ground cardamom
Powdered sugar

Beat egg yolks well. Add sugar; mix well. Add remaining ingredients except powdered sugar. Roll out dough to 1/4-inch thickness; cut into diamond shapes. Make slit in center of each cookie; draw one corner through, making knot. Fry in deep fat at 370 degrees for 2 to 3 minutes or until golden brown. Dust with powdered sugar. Yield: 100 cookies.

Eleanor Ostman
The St. Paul Dispatch-Pioneer Press

FROZEN PLUM PUDDING

5 egg yolks
1/2 c. sugar
1/4 tsp. salt
2 c. milk, scalded
1/2 c. caramelized sugar
2 1/2 c. thin cream
1/2 lb. macaroons, crushed
1/4 c. sherry
3/4 c. finely cut candied fruit
1/2 c. almonds, diced
1/3 c. white raisins

Beat eggs; blend in sugar and salt. Add

a small amount of milk to egg mixture; combine well. Return to milk in top of double boiler. Cook over hot, not boiling, water until thickened. Add caramelized sugar; mix well. Strain and cool. Add macaroons, sherry, candied fruit, almonds and raisins. Pour into refrigerator trays; freeze. A great holiday dessert for those who find the traditional Christmas steamed puddings too heavy.

Helen Civelli Brown
The San Francisco Examiner

MILE-HIGH STRAWBERRY PIE

1 10-oz. pkg. frozen strawberries
1 c. sugar
2 egg whites
1 tbsp. lemon juice
1/8 tsp. salt
1/2 c. whipping cream
1 tsp. vanilla
1 10-in. baked pie shell

Thaw strawberries; mix with sugar, egg whites, lemon juice and salt in large bowl of electric mixer. Beat at medium speed for 15 minutes or until stiff. Whip cream; add vanilla. Fold into strawberry mixture; pile lightly into pie shell. Freeze for several hours or overnight. One and one-half cups crushed fresh strawberries mixed with 1/2 cup sugar may be substituted for frozen strawberries. Let stand for 20 minutes before mixing with remaining ingredients.

Dorothy Neighbors
The Seattle Times

PEARS DE CACAO

12 canned pear halves
3 tbsp. cocoa
1/4 c. sugar
3/4 c. heavy cream
Dash of salt
1/2 tsp. vanilla
1/4 tsp. mint extract

1 tsp. unflavored gelatin
1 tbsp. cold water
1/2 sq. chocolate, melted
1/3 c. creme de cacao

Drain pears well on paper towels. Combine cocoa and sugar; blend in cream. Add salt, vanilla and mint extract. Soften gelatin in cold water; dissolve over hot water. Add to cream mixture; beat for several minutes to spreading consistency. Fill centers and spread cut sides of pears with chocolate mixture. Place pear halves together; chill for 1 hour or longer. Brush melted chocolate on underside of small firm leaves; place in freezer compartment to harden. Place stuffed pear in each of 6 stemmed compotes; pour portion of creme de cacao over each pear. Peel chocolate from leaves; garnish each pear with chocolate leaf. Pear syrup or chocolate sauce may be substituted for creme de cacao, if desired. These look absolutely elegant served in a stemmed goblet. Yield: 6 servings.

Eleanor Ostman
The St. Paul Dispatch-Pioneer Press

BANANAS FOSTER

2 tbsp. butter
4 tsp. brown sugar
2 bananas
Pinch of cinnamon
1 tsp. banana liqueur
1 oz. rum or brandy
Vanilla ice cream

Mix butter and brown sugar in saucepan; cook over medium heat until caramelized. Cut bananas in 4 slices lengthwise. Add to sugar mixture; cook until tender. Add cinnamon and liqueur; stir. Pour rum over top; do not stir. Ignite; spoon over ice cream while flaming. Yield: 4 servings.

Bettye Anding
The New Orleans States-Item

BAKED PLANTAINS

4 tbsp. butter
4 plantains or green-tipped bananas
1/2 c. light brown sugar
2 tbsp. boiling water
1 tsp. lemon juice
Cinnamon to taste

Heat skillet over medium heat; melt butter in skillet. Add plantains; saute until golden, 5 minutes on each side. Place in buttered shallow baking dish. Dissolve sugar in water; mix with butter in skillet. Pour over plantains; sprinkle with lemon juice and cinnamon. Bake in 350-degree oven for 20 minutes, basting once; serve with sauce. Plantains skin should be black and withered-looking when ripe enough to bake. Yield: 4 servings.

Bettye Anding
The New Orleans States-Item

SPUMONI

2 c. milk
1 c. sugar
4 egg yolks
1/4 tsp. almond extract
1 tbsp. citron, chopped fine
3/4 c. sugar
2 tbsp. cornstarch
2 c. milk
1 c. heavy cream
1 tbsp. chopped pistachio nuts
2 drops of green food coloring
2 c. heavy cream
1/2 c. confectioners' sugar
2 tbsp. rum
1/4 c. cocoa

Combine 2 cups milk, 1 cup sugar, egg yolks and almond extract in saucepan. Cook slowly over low heat until thickened. Cool; add citron. Freeze citron mixture in refrigerator tray until mushy, about 2 hours. Combine 3/4 cup sugar, cornstarch and 2 cups milk in saucepan; stir until dissolved. Cook over low heat until thickened. Cool. Whip 1 cup cream until stiff; fold into cooled mixture. Add nuts and coloring; blend well. Freeze green mixture in refrigerator tray until mushy, about 2 hours. Whip 2 cups cream until stiff; fold in remaining ingredients for chocolate mixture. Chill 2 large bombe molds. Spread half the citron mixture evenly over inside of molds to about 1/2-inch thickness. Spoon chocolate mixture in center of molds. Cover with green mixture. Place waxed paper over top; cover molds. Freeze until solid, at least 2 hours. To unmold, place mold in pan of warm water for few seconds; remove cover and waxed paper. Cover with plate; invert.

Yvonne Rothert
The Oregonian

FLAMING ORANGES

4 oranges
3/4 c. orange marmalade
2 tsp. grated fresh orange peel
2 tsp. grated fresh lemon peel
1/2 c. brandy
4 lge. scoops hard-frozen vanilla or
coffee ice cream
Lightly toasted slivered
almonds (opt.)

Peel oranges; section and remove membrane. Melt marmalade over low heat in chafing dish. Add orange sections and grated peels; heat until bubbling. Add brandy; heat until just warm. Ignite; gently spoon flames over oranges until flames die. Spoon over ice cream; sprinkle with almonds. Serve immediately. Yield: 4 servings.

Elaine Tait
The Philadelphia Inquirer

CHOCOLATE VIENNA TORTE

6 egg yolks
1 c. sugar
3/4 c. flour
1 tsp. baking powder
1 tsp. salt
6 egg whites
1/2 tsp. cream of tartar

3/4 c. grated unsweetened chocolate
1 tsp. vanilla
Sweetened whipped cream
Shaved dark chocolate

Beat egg yolks until thick and lemon colored; beat in 1/2 cup sugar. Sift flour, baking powder and salt together; stir into egg yolk mixture. Beat egg whites with cream of tartar until stiff peaks form. Beat in remaining sugar gradually; beat until stiff and glossy. Fold in chocolate and vanilla gently. Fold in egg yolk mixture gently; pour into 2 round 9-inch layer pans lined with greased waxed paper. Bake at 350 degrees for 25 to 30 minutes or until no imprint remains when touched lightly with finger. Remove from pans immediately; remove paper. Cool. Place layers together with whipped cream; top with whipped cream. Garnish with dark chocolate.

Beverly Kees
The Minneapolis Star

CHOCOLATE ANGEL PIE

2 egg whites
1/8 tsp. salt
1/8 tsp. cream of tartar
1/2 c. sifted sugar
1/2 c. finely chopped walnuts or
    pecans
1/2 tsp. vanilla
1 8-oz. pkg. sweet baking
    chocolate
3 tbsp. water
1 tsp. vanilla
1 c. whipping cream, whipped

Beat egg whites with salt and cream of tartar until foamy; add sugar gradually, beating until stiff peaks form. Fold in walnuts and 1/2 teaspoon vanilla. Spread in 8-inch buttered pie pan, building side up to 1/2 inch above pan. Bake at 300 degrees for 50 to 55 minutes; cool. Melt chocolate in water over low heat, stirring constantly; cool. Add 1 teaspoon vanilla; fold into

whipped cream. Pile into meringue shell; chill 2 hours. Yield: 6-8 servings.

Bertha Scott
The Indianapolis News

DATE PUDDING

2 slices bread
2/3 c. packaged diced dates
3 eggs
1/4 c. sugar
1/4 tsp. salt
1/2 tsp. vanilla
2 1/2 c. scalded milk
1/3 c. graham cracker crumbs
3 tbsp. brown sugar
2 tbsp. melted butter or margarine
Sour cream

Cut bread into 1/2-inch cubes; toast lightly in oven. Spread in 1-quart buttered baking dish. Sprinkle dates over bread. Beat eggs lightly; stir in sugar, salt, vanilla and milk. Pour over dates. Place in a pan containing 1 inch hot water. Bake at 350 degrees for 45 minutes. Combine crumbs, brown sugar and butter. Sprinkle over pudding. Bake for 10 minutes longer. Serve warm or cold with dollop of sour cream on each serving. For the holiday season, this is a delicious pudding made with 2/3 cup cubed candied fruits and topped with hard sauce. Yield: 6 servings.

Marian O'Brien
The St. Louis Globe-Democrat

Date Pudding . . . a delicious dessert

SWEDISH PIE

1/4 c. flour
1/4 tsp. salt
1 1/2 tsp. baking powder
3/8 c. sugar
3/8 c. brown sugar
1 egg
3/4 c. chopped apple
1/2 c. chopped nuts
1 qt. vanilla ice cream

Sift flour, salt and baking powder together. Cream sugars with egg; add flour mixture. Fold in apple and nuts; pour into greased and floured 8-inch round or square baking dish. Bake at 350 degrees for 35 minutes; cool. Soften ice cream; spread over top of pie. Freeze. Yield: 6-8 servings.

Bertha Scott
The Indianapolis News

WILD BLACKBERRY PIE

5 c. blackberries
3/4 to 1 c. sugar
4 to 6 tbsp. flour
1/8 tsp. salt
1 recipe pastry for 2-crust 9-in. pie
2 tbsp. butter

Wash and drain blackberries. Blend sugar, flour and salt. Sprinkle several tablespoons sugar mixture over bottom of pastry-lined pan; spread blackberries over sugar mixture. Sprinkle remaining sugar mixture over blackberries; dot with butter. Moisten edge of lower pastry; top with lattice or vented full crust. Press gently to seal. Bake in hot 450-degree oven for 15 minutes. Reduce heat to 350 degrees; bake for 25 to 30 minutes longer or until blackberries are done and crust is lightly browned. The small first-of-the-season blackberries give this pie an unforgettable flavor. Yield: 6-8 servings.

Marjorie Anderson "Mary Cullen"
The Oregon Journal

BLACK BOTTOM PIE

2 c. fine graham cracker crumbs
1/3 c. melted butter or margarine
3 tbsp. sugar
2 c. milk
1 1/2 tbsp. cornstarch
1/4 tsp. salt
1/2 c. sugar
3 eggs, separated
1 1/2 sq. unsweetened chocolate
2 tsp. vanilla
1 envelope unflavored gelatin
1/2 tsp. cream of tartar
1/2 c. sugar
Whipped cream
Shaved unsweetened chocolate

Mix crumbs, butter and 3 tablespoons sugar; press firmly on bottom and side of 9-inch pie pan. Bake at 400 degrees for 5 minutes; cool. Heat milk in heavy saucepan. Mix cornstarch, salt, 1/2 cup sugar and beaten egg yolks; stir in milk slowly. Return mixture to saucepan; cook over low heat, stirring constantly, until thick, about 15 minutes. Melt 1 1/2 squares chocolate; stir into 1 cup cooked mixture. Add 1 teaspoon vanilla; pour into crust. Refrigerate. Soften gelatin in 1/4 cup cold water; stir into remaining hot cooked mixture. Add remaining vanilla; chill. Beat egg whites until foamy; add cream of tartar. Beat egg whites, adding 1/2 cup sugar gradually, until stiff. Fold into gelatin mixture; pour on chocolate layer in crust. Chill for several hours; top with whipped cream and shaved chocolate.

Lillian Marshall
The Louisville Courier-Journal

BROWNIE-BOTTOMED BOURBON PIE

1 pkg. brownie mix
5 egg yolks
3/4 c. sugar
1 envelope unflavored gelatin

1/4 c. cold water
1/2 c. bourbon
1 1/2 c. whipping cream
Dash of salt
Pinch of sugar
2 tbsp. shaved chocolate (opt.)

Prepare brownie mix according to package directions; pour into 10-inch pie pan. Bake according to package directions. Beat egg yolks in electric mixer or by hand until thick and lemon colored; beat in sugar slowly. Soften gelatin in cold water; blend in 3 tablespoons bourbon. Heat over boiling water until gelatin dissolves; pour into egg yolk mixture, stirring briskly. Blend in remaining bourbon. Whip 1 cup cream; fold into bourbon mixture. Pour over baked brownie; chill for at least 4 hours. Whip remaining cream with salt and pinch of sugar; decorate top of pie. Sprinkle with shaved chocolate.

Eleanor Ostman
The St. Paul Dispatch-Pioneer Press

GRAPE PIE

1 c. sifted all-purpose flour
1 3/4 c. sugar
1 tsp. grated lemon peel
1/2 c. butter
1 egg yolk, slightly beaten
1/2 tsp. vanilla
3 lb. Concord grapes
4 tsp. cornstarch
Whipped cream

Combine flour, 1/4 cup sugar and grated peel in bowl; cut in butter till mixture resembles coarse meal. Stir in egg yolk and vanilla; mix with hands till blended. Pat evenly into 9-inch springform pan, building sides up to about 1 inch; chill. Slip skins from grapes; reserve. Place pulp in saucepan; cook over low heat for 15 minutes. Strain to remove seeds; return pulp to saucepan. Add 1/2 cup sugar; cook over low heat for 10 minutes. Mix 1 teaspoon cornstarch with small amount of cold water; stir into grape mixture. Cook, stirring, until slightly thickened; cool for about 10 minutes. Pour into pastry. Bake at 400 degrees for 15 minutes; cool thoroughly. Cook grape skins without water for 15 minutes; put through sieve. Pour juice in saucepan with remaining sugar; cook over low heat for 5 minutes. Mix remaining cornstarch with small amount of cold water; stir into juice mixture. Cook for 1 to 2 minutes or till slightly thickened; cool. Pour over pulp mixture in crust; chill for several hours or overnight. Cut in wedges; serve with whipped cream. Favorite recipe with Concords, so plentiful that Geneva, Ohio, annually stages a festival in their honor and serves dishes like this. Yield: 10-12 servings.

Janet Beighle
The Cleveland Plain Dealer

EGG CUSTARD PIE

4 egg yolks, beaten
3/4 c. sugar
2 c. milk, scalded
1/4 tsp. salt
1 tsp. vanilla
1 unbaked pastry shell
4 egg whites, beaten
1/2 c. sugar

Beat egg yolks well. Combine with 3/4 cup sugar; beat until lemon colored. Pour milk over egg yolk mixture slowly, stirring constantly; add salt and vanilla. Dry pastry shell lightly; pour in egg yolk mixture. Bake for 15 minutes at 400 degrees. Reduce heat to 250 degrees; bake until custard is firm. Beat egg whites until stiff but not dry; beat in 1/2 cup sugar. Place on custard. Bake at 300 degrees until golden brown. Yield: 6-8 servings.

Grace Hartley
The Atlanta Journal

LEMON MERINGUE PIE

1 1/3 c. sugar
6 tbsp. cornstarch
2 1/2 c. cold water
4 eggs, separated
2 tbsp. butter
1 tsp. vanilla
Grated rind of 2 lemons
1/2 c. fresh lemon juice
1 baked 9 or 10-in. pie shell
Pinch of salt
1/4 c. sugar
1/2 tsp. vanilla

Combine 1 1/3 cups sugar, cornstarch and water in medium saucepan; cook until clear and bubbling, stirring constantly with large wire whisk. Add beaten egg yolks, butter and 1 teaspoon vanilla; cook until bubbling. Add lemon rind and lemon juice; stir well. Pour into pie shell. Beat egg whites with salt until creamy; beat, adding 1/4 cup sugar gradually. Add 1/2 teaspoon vanilla; beat until mixture stands in peaks. Spread on pie, smoothing to edge of crust all around. Bake in preheated 250-degree oven until golden brown. Yield: 8 servings.

Jane Benet
The San Francisco Chronicle

MAI TAI PIE

1 1-lb. 4-oz. can crushed
*   pineapple, undrained*
2/3 c. sugar
1/4 c. cornstarch
1/4 tsp. salt
5 eggs, separated
1/4 c. light rum
1 tbsp. butter
1/2 tsp. grated lime peel
1 tsp. lime juice
2/3 c. sugar
1 baked 9-inch pie shell with
*   fluted rim*

Combine pineapple, 2/3 cup sugar, cornstarch and salt. Cook over moderate heat, stirring constantly, until mixture boils and is thick. Beat egg yolks lightly; stir in small amount of hot pineapple mixture. Combine with remaining hot mixture; cook for 1 minute longer over low heat, stirring briskly. Remove from heat; blend in rum, butter, lime peel and lime juice. Beat egg whites until stiff; beat in 2/3 cup sugar gradually, until stiff peaks form. Fold 1 cup beaten egg whites into rum mixture; turn into pie shell. Cover with remaining egg whites. Bake in 350-degree oven for 10 to 15 minutes or until lightly browned; cool. Refreshing dessert, especially in summer; ideal finale for Polynesian feast or luau.

Helen Civelli Brown
The San Francisco Examiner

PECAN PIE

3 eggs
1 c. brown sugar
1 c. dark corn syrup
1 c. broken pecan meats
1 tsp. vanilla
1/2 tsp. salt
1 recipe pastry for 9-in. pie

Beat eggs and sugar together until thick. Add corn syrup, pecan meats, vanilla and salt. Mix well; pour into pastry-lined pie pan. Bake at 300 degrees for about 1 hour or until firm.

Rachel Daniel
The New Orleans Times-Picayune

SENATE RUM PIE

3/4 c. sugar
4 tbsp. cornstarch
1/2 tsp. salt
3 c. milk
4 egg yolks, slightly beaten
1 tbsp. butter
1 1/2 tbsp. dark rum or to taste
1 Graham Cracker Crust
Whipped cream
Chopped nuts

Grasshopper Pie . . . as colorful as it is delicious

Mix sugar, cornstarch and salt in saucepan; stir in milk gradually. Bring to a boil over medium heat, stirring constantly; boil for 1 minute. Stir half the mixture into egg yolks; stir in remaining sugar mixture. Place over medium heat; boil for 1 minute, stirring constantly. Remove from heat; cool slightly. Blend in butter and rum; pour into Graham Cracker Crust. Chill. Top with whipped cream; sprinkle with nuts.

GRAHAM CRACKER CRUST

1 1/2 c. graham cracker crumbs
1/2 c. powdered sugar
1/2 tsp. nutmeg
1/2 c. melted butter or margarine

Mix crumbs, sugar and nutmeg. Add butter; mix thoroughly. Pour into pie tin; press firmly on bottom and side. Chill for at least 20 minutes.

Elinor Lee
The Washington Post

GRASSHOPPER PIE

1 1/2 c. chocolate wafer crumbs
1/4 c. melted butter or margarine
1/4 c. sugar
1 envelope unflavored gelatin
1/3 c. cream
1/4 c. sugar
4 egg yolks, beaten
1/4 c. creme de cacao
1/4 c. green creme de menthe
1 c. heavy cream, whipped

Blend wafer crumbs with butter and 1/4 cup sugar; press into bottom and side of 8 or 9-inch pie pan. Bake at 450 degrees for 5 minutes; cool. Soften gelatin in cream; dissolve over hot water. Beat 1/4 cup sugar into egg yolks. Stir in creme de cacao, creme de menthe and gelatin; chill until slightly thickened. Fold in whipped cream; pour into crumb crust. Chill until firm; sprinkle with additional chocolate wafer crumbs, if desired.

Julie Benell
The Dallas Morning News

117

FLAMING FRIED CREAM

2 tbsp. cornstarch
4 tbsp. flour
1/2 c. sugar
2 c. milk
4 egg yolks, beaten
Dash of nutmeg
Dash of salt
1 tsp. vanilla
Fine cracker crumbs
1 egg, beaten
1/2 c. brandy or maple syrup

Combine cornstarch, flour and sugar in top of double boiler; add milk gradually, stirring constantly. Cook over boiling water until thickened; cook for 5 minutes longer or until starch is cooked, stirring constantly. Stir part of the hot mixture into eggs; pour eggs into hot mixture, stirring constantly. Add nutmeg and salt; cook for about 1 minute longer. Remove from heat; add vanilla. Pour into oiled 8 x 4-inch loaf pan; let stand in refrigerator for 4 to 5 hours or overnight. Cut into 6 strips about the size of 1/4 pound butter sticks. Roll in cracker crumbs. Dip in egg; roll in crumbs again. Fry in deep hot fat at 380 degrees until golden brown. Heat about 1/2 cup brandy; pour over hot fried cream. Light brandy; spoon over cream sticks until flame goes out. Serve at once.

Margaret C. Bowers
The Oakland Tribune

COLD SHERRY SOUFFLE

2 envelopes unflavored gelatin
1 1/2 c. sweet sherry
6 eggs, separated
3/4 c. sugar
1 tbsp. lemon juice
1 c. heavy cream
Ladyfingers

Soften gelatin in 1/2 cup cold water for 5 minutes. Place over boiling water; stir until dissolved. Remove from heat; add sherry. Cool. Chill for 30 minutes or until mixture begins to thicken. Beat egg whites until foamy; add 1/2 cup sugar gradually, beating constantly. Add lemon juice; beat until mixture is stiff but not dry. Beat egg yolks until frothy; add 1/4 cup sugar gradually. Beat until thick and lemon colored. Add slightly thickened wine gelatin slowly to egg yolks; continue beating until thick and light. Fold egg whites into gelatin mixture. Whip cream; fold in. Pour into a collared 7-inch souffle dish lined with ladyfingers. Chill for 3 hours or until firm. Remove paper collar before serving. Serve with additional whipped cream if desired. To make collar for souffle dish, cut strip of waxed paper 6 inches wide and long enough to fit around top of dish. Fold over and make double strip 3 inches wide. Butter one side; tie strip around dish, butter side in, so that it stands like collar above edge. This dessert was served to Dr. Don Manuel Prado, President of Peru, when he was entertained in Colonial Williamsburg at a State dinner given by Winthrop Rockefeller. Yield: 12 servings.

Elinor Lee
The Washington Post

UPSIDE-DOWN DATE PUDDING

1 c. pitted dates, cut up
1 c. boiling water
1/2 c. sugar
1/2 c. brown sugar
1 egg
2 tbsp. butter or margarine
1 1/2 c. sifted flour
1 tsp. baking soda
1/2 tsp. baking powder
1/2 tsp. salt
1 c. chopped walnuts
1 1/2 c. brown sugar

1 tbsp. butter or margarine
1 1/2 c. boiling water

Combine dates and water; cool. Blend sugar, 1/2 cup brown sugar, egg and 2 tablespoons butter. Sift flour, soda, baking powder and salt together; add to sugar mixture. Stir in walnuts and date mixture. Pour into 11 x 7 x 1 1/2-inch baking dish. Combine 1 1/2 cups brown sugar, 1 tablespoon butter and 1 1/2 cups boiling water; pour over pudding. Bake at 375 degrees for 40 minutes. Cut in squares; invert on plate. Serve warm with whipped cream.

Carol Voshall
The Phoenix Gazette

CREAMY OLD-FASHIONED RICE PUDDING

1 qt. milk
1/4 tsp. salt
1/2 c. long grain rice
1/2 c. raisins
1 c. evaporated milk
2 eggs, slightly beaten
1/2 c. sugar
1/2 tsp. vanilla
Nutmeg

Scald milk in saucepan; stir in salt, rice and raisins. Simmer for 20 minutes, stirring occasionally. Combine evaporated milk, eggs, sugar and vanilla with wire whisk; stir into rice mixture. Cook, stirring constantly, for 3 minutes or until slightly thickened. Pour into serving dish, stirring occasionally. Sprinkle top with nutmeg. Serve with cream. Yield: 4 servings.

Alice Petersen
The New York News

COFFEE MALLOW

1 c. strong coffee
27 lge. marshmallows
1 c. heavy cream, whipped stiff

Bring coffee to a boil; remove from heat. Cut marshmallows into quarters; place in hot coffee. Stir until marshmallows melt; cool slightly. Fold in whipped cream; ladle into parfait glasses. Cool for several minutes; refrigerate for at least 4 hours before serving. Yield: 6 servings.

Janice Okun
The Buffalo Evening News

BUTTERSCOTCH SAUCE

1 1/2 c. sugar
1/2 tsp. salt
1 c. golden corn syrup
1/2 c. butter
2 c. cream
1 tsp. vanilla

Boil sugar, salt, syrup, butter and 1 cup cream to soft-ball stage, 230 degrees on candy thermometer. Add remaining cream; cook to 228 degrees on candy thermometer or to desired consistency. Stir in vanilla.

Mary Hart
The Minneapolis Tribune

RASPBERRY CREAM BAVARIAN

1 10-oz. pkg. frozen red raspberries
1 3-oz. pkg. raspberry gelatin
1 c. hot water
1 tbsp. lemon juice
Dash of salt
1 pt. vanilla ice cream
Dessert topping

Thaw and drain raspberries, reserving syrup. Dissolve gelatin in hot water; add reserved syrup, lemon juice and salt. Chill until partially set. Soften ice cream; fold in gelatin mixture. Fold in raspberries. Chill until firm. Serve with dessert topping. Yield: 6-8 servings.

Opal M. Crandall
The San Diego Union

Liquid Refreshers That Cool in Summer
or Warm the Toes of Winter Sportsmen

Beverages give you special opportunities to show
off your imagination and talent as a food
artist. You can serve tangy fruit coolers in the
summer, and warm, spicy drinks in the winter to drive
out the chill from active sledders and ice skaters.

The recipes on the following pages make use of fruit
juices, coffee, tea, chocolate, and other all-time
favorites. These are the beverage recipes which America's leading newspaper food editors think are the very
best. Your family and friends will probably love all of them.

For beautiful beverages you can choose rich Chocolate
Mocha served from chilled glasses; lovely Tropical
Milk Float garnished with mint, spiced Iced Tea with
a whipped honey topping, exotic Brazilian Mocha with
a shaved chocolate garnish, Frosty Sherbet Punch
perfect for parties, tall glasses of Fruited-Tea,
sparkling Golden Punch, sparkling Rhenish Punch,
a superb recipe for Instant Russian Tea, or wine glasses
filled with Spiced Coffee Vienna.

121

BRAZILIAN MOCHA

4 c. strong coffee
2 tbsp. sugar
1/2 c. chocolate syrup
1 pt. coffee ice cream
Shaved chocolate (opt.)

Pour 2 cups coffee in blender with 8 cracked ice cubes; blend at medium speed. Pour 3 ounces iced coffee into 8 glasses. Pour remaining coffee in blender. Add sugar, chocolate syrup and ice cream; blend at high speed. Fill glasses; garnish with shaved chocolate. Yield: 8 servings.

Janice Okun
The Buffalo Evening News

MOCHA VELVA

Chocolate ice cream
Coffee ice cream
Vanilla ice cream
Strong hot coffee
Whipped cream

Fill tall glasses to brim with alternating scoops of chocolate, coffee and vanilla ice cream. Pour coffee into glasses; top each with whipped cream. You will spoon this satiny-smooth cooler at the beginning, but end by sipping through a straw.

Patricia Williams
The Cincinnati Enquirer

SPICED COFFEE VIENNA

3 c. hot strong coffee
2 cinnamon sticks
4 whole cloves
4 allspice berries
Whipped cream
Nutmeg
Sugar

Pour coffee over cinnamon, cloves and allspice; heat over low heat for 10 to 15 minutes. Strain. Pour into table wine glasses; top with whipped cream.

Sprinkle with nutmeg; serve with sugar. Yield: 6 servings.

Elaine Tait
The Philadelphia Inquirer

FROSTY SHERBET PUNCH

3 1-qt. 14-oz. cans orange-
*   grapefruit juice*
3 1-qt. 14-oz. cans pineapple juice
3 12-oz. cans apricot nectar
3 qt. ginger ale
3 qt. lemon sherbet

Chill juices and ginger ale thoroughly. Empty 1 can each juice and 1 quart ginger ale into punch bowl; add 1 quart sherbet. Spoon liquid over sherbet until partially melted; serve. Repeat process, adding another unit of each ingredient, when punch runs low. For a non-alcoholic, easy-to-make punch you can't beat this recipe. It was given to me by my home economics friends at National Canners Association. Yield: 3 gallons.

Elinor Lee
The Washington Post

TEA-FRUIT PUNCH

1/3 c. strong hot tea
1 c. sugar
1 can orange juice concentrate
1/2 c. lemon juice
1 pt. chilled ginger ale
1 pt. club soda
Orange sherbet

Pour hot tea over sugar; stir until sugar is dissolved. Add orange concentrate and lemon juice. Chill. Place ice in bowl or pitcher. Pour orange mixture over top. Add ginger ale and club soda. Top with scoops of orange sherbet at serving time. Yield: About 1 1/2 quarts.

Opal M. Crandall
The San Diego Union

GOLDEN PUNCH

    2   46-oz. cans pineapple juice
    4   6-oz. cans frozen orange juice,
        reconstituted
    3   6-oz. cans frozen lemonade,
        reconstituted
    1   6-oz. can frozen limeade,
        reconstituted
    4 qt. ginger ale, chilled
    2 qt. sparkling water, chilled

Combine all fruit juices; chill. Pour
over ice in punch bowl; add car-
bonated beverages. Yield: 75 servings.

Dorothy Neighbors
The Seattle Times

RHENISH PUNCH

    2 c. sugar
    1 qt. freshly brewed tea
    2 c. lemon juice
    1 qt. orange juice
    6 c. cranberry juice
    1 qt. ginger ale, chilled

Boil sugar with 1 cup water just
until sugar is dissolved; cool. Cool tea.
Pour tea, 2 quarts cold water and remaining ingredients except ginger ale
and sugar syrup into punch bowl. Add
block of ice to bowl just before
serving; pour in ginger ale. Sweeten to
taste with sugar syrup. Yield: 60
punch cup servings.

Marian O'Brien
The St. Louis Globe-Democrat

INSTANT RUSSIAN TEA

    1/2 c. instant tea powder
    2 c. orange-flavored instant
        breakfast drink
    1   3-oz. pkg. imitation-flavored
        lemonade mix
    3/4 c. sugar
    1/2 tsp. cinnamon
    1/2 tsp. allspice
    1/4 tsp. cloves

Golden Punch

Mix all ingredients well. Place 2 or 3
rounded teaspoonfuls in cup; add boiling water. Makes refreshing cold drink
also.

Julie Benell
The Dallas Morning News

VERMONT COOLER

    1 pt. vanilla ice cream
    1 qt. ice cold milk
    1/2 c. maple syrup

Soften ice cream; combine with remaining ingredients. Beat well with
rotary or electric beater; serve ice cold.
Try Vermont Cooler as base for lus-
cious float, using additional pint of ice
cream. Place scoop into each glass;
pour Vermont Cooler over ice cream.
Yield: Twelve 1/2 cup servings.

Janet Christensen
The Boston Herald Traveler

123

Chocolate Mocha

TROPICAL MILK FLOAT

1 c. fresh orange juice, chilled
1 c. pineapple juice, chilled
3/4 c. lime juice, chilled
1/2 tsp. mint flavoring
4 tbsp. sugar
Pinch of salt
Cold milk
6 scoops vanilla ice cream
Fresh mint sprigs or lime wedges

Combine first 6 ingredients; divide evenly into 6 tall glasses. Add cold milk to each slowly, stirring rapidly. Drink will have texture of buttermilk. Top with scoops of ice cream. Garnish with mint. Yield: 6 servings.

Jane Benet
The San Francisco Chronicle

CHOCOLATE MOCHA

3/4 c. chocolate syrup
1 qt. vanilla ice cream, softened
1 1/2 c. milk
1 tbsp. instant coffee
Sweetened whipped cream
Cinnamon

Spoon 3 tablespoons chocolate syrup into 4 chilled glasses. Stir ice cream to soften slightly; blend in milk and coffee. Pour mixture over syrup in glasses. Top with 1 tablespoon whipped cream; add dash of cinnamon. Yield: 4 servings.

Opal M. Crandall
The San Diego Union

SPICED TEA WITH HONEY TOPPING

4 1/2 c. water
1 cinnamon stick
4 whole cloves
2 tbsp. loose tea
2/3 c. dry instant non-dairy
* coffee creamer*
1/3 c. milk
1 1/2 tbsp. sugar
1/2 tsp. vanilla
1 tbsp. honey
2 tbsp. chopped maraschino cherries

Combine water, cinnamon and cloves in saucepan. Bring to a boil; simmer for 10 minutes. Remove from heat. Add tea; cover. Steep for 3 to 5 minutes; strain. Chill bowl and beaters in refrigerator for 15 minutes. Blend coffee creamer, milk, sugar and vanilla in chilled bowl; whip at high speed with electric mixer until soft peaks form, 3 to 5 minutes. Fold in honey and cherries. Serve honey whipped topping on tea. Yield: 4-6 servings.

Cyrilla Riley
The Detroit News

PHOTOGRAPHY CREDITS: California Avocado Advisory Board; National Dairy Council; American Honey Institute; Brussels Sprouts Marketing Program; National Kraut Packers Association; California Strawberry Advisory Board; Standard Brands: Fleischmann's Margarine, Fleischmann's Yeast, Planter's Oil; The Pet Milk Company; National Fisheries Institute; South African Rock Lobster Service Corporation; Ocean Spray Cranberries, Inc.; United Fresh Fruit and Vegetable Association; National Livestock and Meat Board; Olive Administrative Committee; International Tuna Fish Association; The Nestle Company; Chiffon Margarine; Knox Gelatine, Inc.; American Lamb Council; McIlhenny Company (Tabasco); California Raisin Advisory Board; The Borden Company; National Macaroni Institute.